PRAISE FOR

EASY PLANT-BASED
Cooking for Two

"Lei has cultivated such a fresh, authentic, and utterly inviting take on cooking up wholesome, satisfying plant-based recipes for two, you won't be able to wait to charge into the kitchen with her fabulous book."

—Sharon Palmer, the Plant-Powered Dietitian

"Lei offers a guide to plant-based eating that's approachable, fun, and delicious. This book is full of back-pocket, big-flavor recipes that everyone from the baker to the meal prepper will return to again and again."

—Lizzy Briskin, Food Editor at *Real Simple*

"Lei shares a colorful collection of delicious plant-based dishes. This book is destined to make your taste buds happy and become a cherished kitchen companion!"

—Evelisse Capó, PharmD, DipACLM

"Lei Shishak's *Easy Plant-Based Cooking for Two* is a beautiful cookbook that combines delectable, nutrient-dense foods in imaginative ways to produce the most delicious meals for two. Discover Nut & Seed Granola, Apple Oatcakes, One-Bowl Breakfast Cookies, Jackfruit Burritos, and more—all made with simple, wholesome ingredients."

—Kim Campbell, chef, and author of *PlantPure Nation*, *PlantPure Kitchen*, and *PlantPure Comfort Food*

"This cookbook is a real page-turner, with so many vibrant recipes everywhere you turn! I love the use of fresh herbs and spices in many of the recipes, which not only enhances the flavor, but also the health benefits of each dish. From Asian-inspired cuisine to Italian, your taste buds will not get bored. Even if you don't follow a vegan diet, you will find ways to incorporate these vegetable-forward recipes into your life."

—April Murray-Kelly, RDN Owner of OC Nutrition Coaching

"Breaking down the barrier between 'plant-based food' and 'everyday food,' Lei Shishak proves that a meal without meat is far from lacking. In fact, you could easily flip through the pages of *Easy Plant-Based Cooking for Two* and be drawn in by her skill at melding fresh ingredients, vibrant flavors, and common staples without once thinking about veganism. Written through the lens of an omnivore, it's an excellent resource for anyone seeking healthier options, whether you're all-in for a dietary overhaul or not. At the end of the day, it's just great food, period."

—Hannah Kaminsky, author of *Real Food Really Fast*, *The Student Vegan Cookbook*, and many more

EASY PLANT-BASED
Cooking for Two

Delicious Vegan Recipes to Enjoy Together

LEI SHISHAK

author of *Farm-to-Table Desserts* and *Beach House Baking*

Skyhorse Publishing

Library of Congress Cataloging-in-Publication Data is available on file.

Cover design by David Ter-Avanesyan
Cover photo credit by Lei Shishak
Interior design and layout by Chris Schultz

Print ISBN: 978-1-5107-7208-3
Ebook ISBN: 978-1-5107-7209-0

Printed in China

To my readers—

There are a lot of cookbooks out there. That is why it means so much to me that you chose mine. I hope you enjoy making my recipes—or using them as inspiration for your creations. May these recipes tickle your taste buds, satisfy your cravings, and open your eyes to the wonderful world of plant-based eating.

shishak

farm-to-table desserts

LEI SHISHAK Beach House DINNERS

Beach House Brunch Lei Shishak

Shishak

Beach House Baking

CONTENTS

INTRODUCTION

Hello! If you're reading this, you're likely interested in joining the plant-based movement and making some exciting changes to your eating habits. Or perhaps you've already made the change and are looking for new recipes to add to your repertoire. Or maybe you're an empty-nester craving healthy meals to share with your favorite plus-one. Whatever the case may be, I'm so glad you're here.

It's hard to ignore the momentum toward plant-based eating. Pandemic-driven meat shortages, financial strains, environmental concerns, and a desire to eat healthier have collectively increased the demand for plant-based foods. Many restaurants even highlight plant-based dishes on their menu, and grocery stores carry a wide range of plant-based meat alternatives.

I grew up in a meat-eating household. We ate meat for breakfast, lunch, and dinner. Heck, we even snacked on meat (homemade jerky, anyone?). Attending culinary school and working as a professional chef didn't change this. I became more dependent on meat. You see, chefs have some of the worst diets. We get off work late, leave work famished, and crave fast, cheap, fried food. Chicken wings, pulled pork nachos, and beef burgers were my late-night foods of choice.

The start of the 2020 pandemic was the catalyst for my plant-based journey. For years, I had wanted to eat healthier but always put it off. Now homebound, I knew it was a perfect time. After researching different diets and learning about the detrimental effects of the standard American diet—obesity, heart disease, diabetes, skyrocketing medical costs, a dying planet—it became clear that a plant-based diet was the right choice.

Plant-based or plant-forward eating focuses on foods primarily from plants. It doesn't necessarily mean you are vegetarian or vegan and never eat meat or dairy. Rather, you eat more nutrient-dense plants, less meat, less processed foods, and more fiber. It's a way of eating that is totally doable, improves health, lowers grocery bills, and helps the planet.

I decided to develop all the recipes in this cookbook to be meat-free and vegan. However, if you're eating meat and dairy, go ahead and add shrimp to the pasta cacciatore, a slather of butter on the garlic naan, or a soft-boiled egg to the ramen. Remember that the goal is to eat more vegetables and less meat. After cooking and eating the simple, good-for-you recipes in *Easy Plant-Based* *Cooking for Two*, you'll begin to see the extraordinary impact food has on the health of our bodies, our communities, and our planet.

As I continue each day to look for environmentally sustainable options in my life, it made sense to develop the recipes for small-batch cooking. Over 60 percent of households in the United States consist of one or two people (*Statista 2021*). All the recipes are

perfectly portioned for these smaller house-holds, but also work for larger households where varied eating preferences often exist.

Small-batch cooking isn't complicated or restrictive. It cuts down on waste (and waist!) and leads to greater variety in meals. So whether you're newly married, flying solo, BFFs, roommates, empty-nesters, or one in a large crowd, get ready to say goodbye to endless leftovers and hello to a new, deli-cious, plant-based dish every day.

Have the BEST day!

ALL ABOUT PLANT-BASED EATING

What is it?

Plant-based eating is more than just a diet—it's a lifestyle focused on eating foods that come directly from nature, specifically: fruits, vegetables, seeds, nuts, legumes, beans, and whole grains. Every time you step in the grocery store, your goal should be to buy the most unprocessed, natural foods possible. Processed foods have additives and chemicals detrimental to our bodies.

Being plant-based doesn't necessarily mean you are full-blown vegan. Perhaps you eat fish, but your plant-based friend steers clear for environmental concerns. Maybe you pass on honey for ethical reasons, but your partner can't get enough of it. You draw the line where you see fit—deciding what works for you while eating the majority of food from plants. I always start my day by asking myself, "How can I eat healthier today by adding more plant-based foods to my plate?"

WHAT ARE THE PROS?

Our bodies thrive on plant-based diets. Numerous studies show that overall health improves because of the added fiber, minerals, vitamins, and protein from plant foods. Plant-based eating also positively affects the environment.

- *Reduces inflammation.* Plants are abundant in anti-inflammatory nutrients that strengthen the immune system.

- *Maintains heart health and lowers blood pressure.* Plants are low in saturated fats, keeping cholesterol levels down.

- *Lowers risk of certain cancers.* Phytonutrients found in plants help eliminate free radicals and protect against cellular damage.

- *Prevents type-2 diabetes*. Plant-based diets are high in fiber and antioxidants, which help regulate blood sugar. Also, plants are low in saturated fat, leading to less fatty tissue to interfere with insulin absorption.

- *Lowers weight*. Plant-based diets are rich in low glycemic foods that maintain blood sugar levels, keeping us feeling full longer.

- *Supports digestive health*. Plant-based foods—whole grains, legumes, nuts, seeds, fruits, vegetables—are high in fiber and gut-friendly bacteria.

- *Conserves environment*. Eating more plant-based foods can lead to reducing the carbon footprint of the livestock industry (e.g., methane emissions, chemical fertilizers, and pesticides).

- *Minimizes animal cruelty*. Eating more plant-based foods lowers the demand for animal products, which reduces animals being raised for slaughter.

- *Lessens time in the kitchen*. Plant-based foods cook faster—or just as fast—as animal products. Many plants can be eaten raw, as well.

- *Saves money*. Bulk, dried, and canned items are budget friendly. Buy fresh produce only in amounts you need.

- *Prolongs life*. A welcome by-product of the aforementioned benefits!

WHAT ARE THE CONS?

There are potential risks when you omit animal products from your diet, especially if you are vegan. What matters most is that you are aware of them and know how to prevent them from happening.

- *Protein deficiencies.* Many plant-based proteins are incomplete proteins, meaning they do not contain all nine essential amino acids our bodies need. Focus on eating a varied diet of complete proteins (like soy and quinoa) and high-protein plant foods (see **My Top 10 High-Protein Plant Foods**).

- *Nutrient deficiencies. Vitamin B12* Plants lack B12, so eat fortified foods, soy, and nutritional yeast to prevent anemia—or take a supplement. *Iron* Our bodies do not easily absorb plant-based iron (non heme). Combine iron-rich lentils, spinach, and chickpeas with vitamin C-rich citrus, bell peppers, and broccoli to enhance absorption. *Calcium* Focus on eating dark, leafy vegetables high in calcium along with mushrooms, which boost absorption. *Omega 3 fatty acids* Eat flax, chia, and walnuts—or consider adding small amounts of fish like mackerel, salmon, anchovies, and sardines to your diet.

- *Perishable produce.* Fresh produce doesn't last long. Buy only what you need to prevent waste.

MY TOP 10 HIGH-PROTEIN PLANT FOODS

These are my favorite sources of plant-based protein:

- Lentils
- Soy (tofu, tempeh, edamame)
- Chickpeas
- Peanut butter
- Almonds
- Pumpkin seeds
- Quinoa
- Flax seeds
- Kidney beans
- Hemp seeds

You can take different approaches to a plant-based diet. *You* decide which level is best for you and your health goals.

- *Vegetarian.* May consume animal products, such as eggs and dairy, but does not eat meat such as beef, chicken, and pork.

- *Pescatarian.* Adds seafood to the vegetarian diet.

- *Flexitarian.* Consumes mostly plant foods supplemented by small amounts of animal products.

- *Vegan.* No consumption of any animal products (e.g., eggs, honey, dairy, meat, seafood) or any foods that may have inflicted harm on an animal during the production process. Vegans also exclude animal products from their everyday lives. They do not wear animal skins such as leather and wool and may avoid events that offer animal attractions.

- *Raw Vegan.* Follows the vegan diet and lifestyle and eats only raw, plant-based foods.

- *Whole Food Plant-Based.* Consumes no animal products (e.g., eggs, honey, dairy, meat, seafood). This diet is considered a vegan diet with an emphasis on health. Oils and overly processed foods high in fat, sugar, and salt are omitted.

TIPS FOR STARTING A PLANT-BASED DIET

Okay, so you've decided to go plant-based. Now what? Transitioning to a plant-based diet can be as big or small a deal as you want it to be, and as mentioned earlier, there are different levels of plant-based eating. Whichever path you choose, you'll be successful if you have the right attitude and approach it thoughtfully. Here are some tips that may help you on your plant-based journey:

1. *Determine your motivation.* Ask yourself, why am I doing this? Is it for health reasons, environmental causes, ethical concerns, etc.?

2. *Find a support system.* We live in a time where we don't have to do anything alone anymore. If you can't find a friend to support you, use an app or join an online group.

3. *Stock your pantry.* Canned goods like beans or frozen fruits and vegetables are great to have on hand. You're less likely to stray if you have food items within arm's reach.

4. *Meal prep when possible.* Convenience is a big factor in success. You're less likely to grab a burger on your way home from work if you know dinner is almost ready.

5. *Stick to familiar flavors and preparations.* For example, don't start day 1 with a tofu egg scramble and cashew cheese sauce; instead, opt for eggless French toast with coconut whipped cream and fresh berries.

6. *View meat as a side dish.* This mental switch is a good way to begin acclimating to eating less meat.

7. *Try out a plant-based meal service.* Stress is an inherent part of dieting. Meal deliveries can help you get over the initial intimidation.

8. *Start with Meatless Mondays.* This one day off from meat is a popular way to ease into plant-based eating.

9. *Or, eat one plant-based meal a day.* I found lunch to be the easiest—when a simple salad or vegetable sandwich was preferred.

10. *Or, limit meat to one meal a day.* Try also eliminating different meats, one at a time.

PLANT-BASED PANTRY

A well-stocked pantry helps you eat healthier and stick to a plant-based diet. These are items that I regularly keep in my pantry. This is by no means an exhaustive list. Use this as a guide; everyone's pantry will be slightly different because we all have different tastes, preferences, and budgets.

Grains: wild rice, brown rice, white rice, quinoa, farro, oats, whole grain bread

Legumes: green lentils, black lentils, red lentils, chana, chickpeas, kidney beans, black beans, tofu, tempeh, edamame

Pasta and Flour: whole wheat pasta, pasta alternatives (e.g., brown rice, cassava), soba noodles, udon noodles, whole wheat flour, all-purpose flour, rye flour, chickpea flour, coconut flour, oat flour, almond flour, gluten-free flour

Nuts and Seeds: almonds, pistachios, peanuts, cashews, nut butters, flax, chia, hemp, sesame, sunflower, pumpkin, seed butters, tahini, seed crackers

Fruits and Vegetables: fresh fruit, dried fruit, frozen fruit, canned fruit, fresh vegetables, frozen vegetables, fresh herbs, dried herbs

Condiments and Sauces: vinegars (apple cider, red wine, white wine, white, rice, champagne), oils (olive, sunflower, canola, grapeseed, avocado, coconut), mustards, salsas, hot sauces, fruit preserves, olives, pepperoncinis, chilies in adobo sauce, liquid coconut aminos, soy sauce, tamari, nutritional yeast, vegetable broth, pickles, vegan Worcestershire

Spices: dried thyme, dried rosemary, dried basil, bay leaf, peppercorns, salts, cayenne pepper, paprika, smoked paprika, Old Bay, garlic powder, celery seed, celery salt, chili powder, curry powder, ground cumin, ground ginger, nutmeg, cinnamon, cloves, coriander, fennel, mustard seeds, nori, dried oregano, red pepper flakes, turmeric

Baking and Sweeteners: baking powder, baking soda, dark chocolate, organic cane sugar, beet sugar, coconut sugar, maple syrup, applesauce, nondairy yogurt, shredded coconut, vegan butter, vanilla extract, almond extract, lemon extract, frozen bananas, canned pumpkin, agave, molasses, cornstarch, tapioca starch, cocoa powder

Beverages: coffee, tea, sparkling water, coconut water, liquor, wine, beer, almond milk, coconut milk, oat milk

Suggested Kitchen Equipment: wooden cutting board, high-powered blender, nonstick cookware, cast-iron pan, small and large baking tray, 6-inch cake pan, 8-ounce ramekins, muffin pan, loaf pan, strainer, food processor, silicone mat, Microplane, mixer, mandoline, bowls, measuring cups and spoons, mortar and pestle, immersion blender, garlic press

Tip: Shop at your local restaurant supply store for deals on kitchen supplies and top-of-the-line equipment.

GROCERY SHOPPING TIPS

These are plant-based foods that you should focus on when grocery shopping.

Vegetables. Pick a variety of colorful vegetables, including leafy greens like kale and collards. There's nothing wrong with buying pre-cut vegetables, too. Remember that convenience is a key factor in success!

Fruits. Choose whole fruits, especially those in season.

Breads and Grains. When shopping for bread, look for fiber, 100-percent whole grain, and low saturated fat. Experiment with different grains like kamut, millet, spelt, quinoa, and oats.

Canned Goods. Look for items with no added oil or sugar and low sodium.

Pastas. Avoid pastas made with refined flours like semolina. Instead, choose 100-percent whole grain pastas—or pasta made with alternatives like brown rice, quinoa, lentil, and cassava.

Nuts and Seeds. Nuts and seeds have a relatively long shelf life, so keep a variety on hand. They make a quick, healthy snack and are great additions to salads and smoothies.

Spices. This is where the fun begins! Experiment with different spices used in global cuisines. Once you find spices you like, buy them in bulk.

Frozen. Stick to the frozen fruit and vegetables. Pass on everything else.

Condiments. Stock up on basics like maple syrup, mustard, tamari, soy sauce, vinegars, and oils.

Refrigerated. Pick up nut milks, seed milks, non-dairy yogurts, non-dairy butter, and non-dairy cheese.

ADDITIONAL TIPS

- Memorize the aisle numbers that carry plant-based foods and visit only those aisles.
- Limit temptation by steering clear of the meat department.
- If buying prepackaged items, choose ones with fewer than five ingredients—and make sure you recognize them.

FAQs

Can I drink alcohol?

Yes, but do so in moderation as in all other aspects of eating.

Is eating plant-based expensive?

Contrary to popular belief, eating plant-based foods is not expensive. The myth stems from three factors: 1) the high price of processed vegan foods like vegan burgers and sausages, 2) the low price of processed foods made with US government-subsidized wheat and corn, and 3) the high cost of maintaining the freshness of perishable produce.

By focusing on plant-based, minimally processed foods, I've cut my food bills in half. Here are some of my money-saving tips:

- Shop seasonal produce; buy frozen if not.
- Use your freezer to store ingredients and meals. Low-moisture vegetables like greens beans, cauliflower, carrots, and winter greens freeze well. Check out the National Center for Home Food Preservation for how to properly freeze food.
- Buy dry essentials—like flour, beans, nuts, seeds, and pastas—in bulk.
- Plan your meals each week so you can see where to save time and money by reusing ingredients in different ways.
- Write a grocery list so you're able to stick to the plan and resist the urge to buy items you don't need.
- Ask yourself, do I really need this? Remember that every food item you buy should have a purpose.
- Batch cook staples like beans, potatoes, rice, and lentils (see next FAQ).

Is batch cooking worth it?

You batcha (sorry)! Batch cooking will save you time and money. While it does require a little planning, it saves you time during the week, guarantees you a healthy meal ready to go, and helps you stay on course when tempted to stray.

Batch cooking can be approached a few different ways:

- Cook all meals for the entire week on just one day
- Cook large batches of staples like rice or beans at one time
- Double recipes to have meals you can freeze

Help! I'm throwing away a lot of fresh produce.

Buy vegetables with a longer shelf life such as celery, carrots, cabbage, romaine lettuce, kale, squash, sweet potatoes, onions, parsley, garlic, broccoli, and cauliflower. If your refrigerator has a crisper drawer, use it to prolong the freshness of these items by storing them at the right humidity.

Will I end up eating the same boring vegetables every day?

There are so many different vegetables out there for you to choose from. As long as you're not a picky eater, you'll end up eating a greater variety than you did before.

Am I going to get enough protein?

YES! By eating the right combination of plant-based protein sources throughout the day, your body will have everything it needs. The recommended dietary allowance to prevent deficiency for an average sedentary adult is 0.36 grams of protein per pound of body weight. For example, a person who weighs 130 pounds should consume approximately 46 grams of protein a day.* Just one (1-ounce) serving of soy provides 23 grams of protein—so you can see that meeting protein requirements is totally doable. Keep in mind, too, that our highest protein requirements occurred during infancy.

The average sedentary man should eat about 56 grams of protein per day, and the average woman should eat about 46 grams.

What is nutritional yeast?

Also referred to as nooch, nutritional yeast is a deactivated form of baker's yeast. It comes in the form of yellow flakes and, when added to food, provides a savory, nutty, cheezy, umami flavor. Nutritional yeast is a good source of vitamin B12, which plants lack.

Is cooking with oil allowed?

Oils are included in plant-based diets. However, there are different approaches to plant-based eating. In the whole food plant-based diet, oils are omitted. For optimum health—and especially if you suffer from heart-related illnesses—you should try to cook with little or no oil.

Ultimately, you determine if oil works with your health goals. I choose to cook with oil in our household, while always looking for opportunities to reduce oil consumption.

- *Invest in nonstick cookware.* Look for heavy-bottomed nonstick pots and pans for even heat distribution. Enamel-coated cast-iron and ceramic titanium pans are also good choices.

- *Invest in nonstick bakeware.* Purchase ceramic bakeware, silicone ovenware, and parchment.

- *Cook on low heat.* Reduces the chance of burning. If scorching or sticking occurs, add water, cooking wine, or vegetable broth one tablespoon at a time.

- *Have mise en place ready.* "Mise en place" is all of the required items to prepare what you make. You'll be less likely to grab a bottle of oil in a panic should any scorching occur.

- *Use a small misting bottle.* Mist with water or vegetable broth while cooking to prevent burning.

- *Steam your foods.* This simple method of cooking requires no oil and retains much of the nutrients in food.

- *Use the broiler.* Browns and crisps, while adding flavor.

- *Invest in an air fryer.* This ingenious piece of equipment has revolutionized oil-free cooking.

- *Use oil substitutes when baking.* Replace oil with ingredients like applesauce and mashed banana. See page 32 for more ideas.

- *Replace oil in salad dressings.* Experiment with mashed avocado, tahini, soaked cashews, mashed cannellini beans, and hot water thickened with cornstarch.

JUST A NOTE ABOUT SOME OF THE INGREDIENTS USED IN THESE RECIPES.

- *Salt.* I use kosher unless otherwise specified.
- *Sugar.* I use organic, unrefined cane sugar unless otherwise specified.
- *Brown sugar.* If not specified, use either light or dark.
- *Rye flour.* I use medium rye.
- *Pepper.* Refers to freshly ground black pepper.
- *Cremini mushrooms.* Also known as Baby Bella.
- *Parsley.* Refers to Italian flat-leaf parsley.
- *Applesauce.* Refers to unsweetened applesauce.
- *Miso.* I use white miso paste.
- *Onion.* Refers to brown or yellow onions unless otherwise specified.

JUST A NOTE ABOUT THESE RECIPES.

Recipes have been marked as gluten-free and oil-free when applicable. Keep in mind that many of the sandwich and pasta recipes can easily be made gluten-free by using gluten-free breads and pastas. All of the recipes were developed using nonstick pots and pans unless otherwise indicated.

REFRESHING BEVERAGES

Beverages are a convenient and versatile way to enjoy the health benefits of plants. We can puree them in juices and smoothies or add their extracts and oils to water, tea, and coffee. Also, thanks to the proliferation of milk alternatives, we can easily drink beverages traditionally made with dairy.

The refreshing plant-based beverages in this chapter are all simple to make and can be enjoyed any time of day. Get ready to feel closer to nature, improve your mood, calm your senses, and naturally energize.

Milk Tea

21

Rooibos Chai

22

Lavender Coffee

25

Bluecado Smoothie

26

Kiwi Kale Smoothie

29

Tropical Smoothie

30

MILK TEA

GLUTEN-FREE | OIL-FREE | YIELD: 2 SERVINGS

If you're a tea-drinker like me, you will love this smooth, refreshing beverage. The almond milk provides calories, carbs, and protein that leave you satiated and energized. Make sure to use fortified almond milk for an added boost of calcium and vitamins A, D, and E.

DIRECTIONS

In a small pot, bring the water to a boil over high heat. Turn off heat, stir in the tea, and steep 4 minutes. Strain the tea into a 2-cup liquid measure and stir in the maple syrup. Chill the tea in the refrigerator for at least 20 minutes.

Fill two (16-ounce) glasses with ice. Divide the tea and milk between the glasses and serve.

> Herbal twist: Whenever I have extra basil on hand, I add some bruised leaves to the tea while it steeps. The oils release and lend sweet, clove-like flavors while providing health benefits like enhanced mood, clearer skin, and improved digestion.

INGREDIENTS

1½ cups filtered water
2–3 tablespoons loose
    black tea*
1 teaspoon maple syrup
ice
1 cup almond milk

* The amount will vary between light and dark teas. I like to use 2 tablespoons Taj Mahal Orange Pekoe tea. It's spicy, smoky, rich, and malty!

ROOIBOS CHAI

GLUTEN-FREE | OIL-FREE | YIELD: 2 SERVINGS

INGREDIENTS

7 cardamom pods

7 cloves

2 black peppercorns

1 (2-inch) cinnamon stick

1 (1-inch) piece peeled
    ginger (about ¼ ounce)

⅛ teaspoon anise seeds

2 cups filtered water

2 rooibos tea bags*

½ cup almond milk

1 tablespoon coconut
    sugar

I like Harney & Sons.

Rooibos tea is a caffeine-free beverage made from the leaves of the South African rooibos bush. It has a gorgeous burnt-red color and a sweet, woody flavor that's perfect for chai. Brewed with aromatic spices of cardamom, clove, peppercorn, cinnamon, ginger, and anise, rooibos chai is spicy, soothing, and warming.

DIRECTIONS

Coarsely grind the cardamom, cloves, peppercorns, cinnamon, ginger, and anise seeds in a mortar and pestle. Transfer to a small pot and cover with 2 cups filtered water. Place over high heat and bring to a rolling boil. Reduce heat and simmer for 3 minutes. Add the tea bags, cover, and continue to simmer for 4 minutes. Turn off heat and stir in the milk and coconut sugar. Strain into two cups and serve.

LAVENDER COFFEE

GLUTEN-FREE | OIL-FREE | YIELD: 2 SERVINGS

Lavender is well-known for its ability to reduce stress and anxiety. With this delicious, infused coffee, you get the calming properties of lavender and the benefits of caffeine without the jitteriness.

DIRECTIONS

Place the coffee grounds and dried lavender in a French press. Boil 2 cups filtered water and fill the press. Cover with the lid and lower the plunger to the surface of the water. Let sit for 5 minutes.

Slowly press down the filter and pour the coffee into two cups. If using, warm the almond milk in a small pot over medium heat (or a microwave) and serve alongside the coffee.

INGREDIENTS

¼ cup coarsely ground dark roast coffee

1 teaspoon dried lavender

2 cups filtered water

1 cup almond milk (optional)

BLUECADO SMOOTHIE

GLUTEN-FREE | OIL-FREE | YIELD: 2 SERVINGS

INGREDIENTS

1 small avocado, halved
  and pitted
1 frozen banana
1½ cups frozen
  blueberries
1 cup baby spinach, lightly
  packed
¾ cup almond milk
½ cup filtered water
½ teaspoon flax seeds

This thick and creamy smoothie is made with blueberries, avocado, banana, spinach, and flax seeds—all blended into a luscious beverage. Packed with powerful antioxidants and absolutely no added sugar, this smoothie makes a great healthy breakfast shake or daytime snack.

DIRECTIONS

Scoop out the avocado flesh and place in a blender. Add the banana, blueberries, spinach, milk, water, and flax seeds. Mix on high for 20 seconds until smooth. Pour into two glasses and serve.

KIWI KALE SMOOTHIE

GLUTEN-FREE | OIL-FREE | YIELD: 2 SERVINGS

This green smoothie combines kiwi and kale—two nutritional powerhouses high in vitamins, minerals, antioxidants, and dietary fiber. It's a delicious way to detox, improve your heart health, and boost immunity in one delicious serving. I like to have this smoothie in the morning or as a mid-afternoon pick-me-up.

DIRECTIONS

Place all the ingredients in a blender. Mix on high for 20 seconds until smooth. Pour into two glasses and serve.

INGREDIENTS

3 ripe kiwis, peeled

1 navel orange, peeled

1½ cups torn kale leaves, loosely packed

1 cup filtered water

1½ teaspoons lemon juice

1½ teaspoons maple syrup

TROPICAL SMOOTHIE

GLUTEN-FREE | OIL-FREE | YIELD: 2 SERVINGS

INGREDIENTS

1 navel orange, peeled
1 cup frozen pineapple
  chunks
1 cup frozen mango
  chunks
1 cup coconut water
1 tablespoon lemon juice
4 deglet noor dates,
  chopped

No need to travel when you can make this delicious tropical smoothie at home! You'll get your fill of tropic flavors from orange, pineapple, mango, lemon, and coconut water. Sweetened naturally with dates, this healthy smoothie is packed with vitamin C, fiber, and potassium.

DIRECTIONS

Place all the ingredients in a blender. Mix on high for 20 seconds until smooth. Pour into two glasses and serve.

HERE'S A HELPFUL GUIDE TO VEGAN-IZING BAKED GOODS.

*Keep in mind that the substitution formulas can vary depending on the
type of baked good and the other ingredients in the recipe.*

Egg substitutes

1 egg = 1 tablespoon flaxseed meal + 3 tablespoons warm water

1 egg = 1 tablespoon chia seeds + 2 tablespoons warm water

1 egg = 1 teaspoon baking soda + 1 tablespoon white vinegar

1 egg = ¼ cup plant-based yogurt

1 egg = ¼ cup fruit puree (e.g., applesauce, mashed banana, pumpkin puree)

1 egg = 2 tablespoons starch (e.g., cornstarch, tapioca) + 3 tablespoons water

1 egg = 3 tablespoons aquafaba

1 egg white = 2 tablespoons aquafaba

1 egg yolk = 1 tablespoon aquafaba

1 egg = 1 teaspoon oil + 2 teaspoons baking powder + 2 tablespoons water

Dairy substitutes

Nut milk, nut butter, oat milk, coconut milk, vegan butter, vegetable oils, applesauce, pureed dates, dairy-free yogurt, mashed banana, mashed avocado

Vegan sweeteners

Organic, unrefined, natural or raw cane sugar, beet sugar, coconut sugar, date sugar, maple syrup, date syrup, brown rice syrup, agave nectar, molasses

AMAZING BAKES

When I first went plant-based, I thought it would be a huge struggle to bake without eggs and dairy—and that taste would surely be compromised. To my pleasant surprise, I was wrong. With some basic substitutions (and a good bit of trial and error), I created some amazing baked treats that I'm happy to share with you in this chapter.

MORNING COFFEE CAKES

YIELD: 2 CAKES

Start your morning with these delightfully sweet coffee cakes. They're light, incredibly tender, and topped with a buttery cinnamon streusel that's impossible to resist. This is egg- and dairy-free baking at its finest.

DIRECTIONS

Preheat oven to 350°F. Lightly grease two (8-ounce) ramekins and set aside.

MAKE STREUSEL:

In a small bowl, stir together 2 tablespoons melted butter and 2 tablespoons brown sugar. Mix in the flour, cinnamon, and salt until it resembles thick, wet sand and set aside.

MAKE CAKE:

In a medium bowl, combine the flours, cinnamon, baking powder, baking soda, and salt and set aside.

In a large bowl, whisk 2 tablespoons butter, sugar, vinegar, and vanilla until combined. Add the almond milk and dry ingredients a little at a time, whisking after each addition until smooth. Divide the batter between the ramekins and crumble the streusel on top.

Bake for 22 minutes or until an inserted toothpick comes out clean. Cool for 15 minutes, then run a paring knife around the edges and flip out the cakes. Garnish with powdered sugar before serving.

STREUSEL

2 tablespoons vegan unsalted butter, melted
2 tablespoons brown sugar
¼ cup all-purpose flour
½ teaspoon cinnamon
pinch of salt

CAKE

½ cup all-purpose flour
2 tablespoons almond flour, sifted
½ teaspoon cinnamon
½ teaspoon baking powder
⅛ teaspoon baking soda
⅛ teaspoon salt
2 tablespoons vegan unsalted butter, melted
2 tablespoons sugar
1½ teaspoons white vinegar
1 teaspoon vanilla extract
½ cup almond milk
powdered sugar for garnish

PUMPKIN BREAD

OIL-FREE | YIELD: 2 SERVINGS

INGREDIENTS
¼ cup all-purpose flour

¼ cup whole wheat flour

¼ cup almond flour,
    sifted

1 teaspoon baking soda

½ teaspoon cinnamon

¼ teaspoon nutmeg

¼ teaspoon salt

⅛ teaspoon baking
    powder

⅛ teaspoon cloves

½ cup pure pumpkin

¼ cup sugar

3 tablespoons water

2 tablespoons applesauce

1½ teaspoons vinegar

½ teaspoon vanilla
    extract

1 teaspoon pepitas

This pumpkin bread is a fantastic way to welcome fall. And using ramekins means you don't need to bake a whole loaf! Made with warm spices of cinnamon, nutmeg, and clove, this classic autumn treat bakes up perfectly moist and flavorful.

DIRECTIONS
Preheat oven to 350°F. Lightly grease two (8-ounce) ramekins and set aside.

In a medium bowl, whisk the flours, baking soda, cinnamon, nutmeg, salt, baking powder, and cloves together.

In a large bowl, whisk the pumpkin, sugar, water, applesauce, vinegar, and vanilla until smooth. Add the dry ingredients to the wet and whisk until combined. Transfer the batter to the prepared ramekins. Sprinkle the tops with pepitas. Press the nuts down slightly so they stick to the batter.

Bake for 22 minutes or until an inserted toothpick comes out clean. Let sit for 10 minutes before inverting onto a wire rack to cool.

RYE RAISIN SCONES

YIELD: 2 SCONES

These rye scones have the perfect balance of sweet and earthy goodness. Wholesome rye flour imparts a nutty, malty flavor and rich color. Filled with juicy raisins and topped with a sweet vanilla glaze, these scones are simply delish.

MAKE SCONES:

Preheat oven to 400°F. Line a baking tray with parchment and set aside.

In a large bowl, combine the flours, baking powder, baking soda, cinnamon, and salt. Add the butter and use a pastry cutter to break it down into pea-sized pieces. Mix in the raisins and place the bowl in the freezer for 5 minutes.

In a small bowl, combine the milk, applesauce, maple syrup, and vinegar and stir to combine (mixture will curdle). Pour over the dry ingredients and mix with your hand until dough comes together.

Transfer dough to a clean counter and shape into a 1-inch-thick rectangle (about 3×5 inches). Use a sharp knife to diagonally slice into two triangles. Transfer to the prepared baking tray and bake for 13 minutes or until the centers bounce back when gently pressed. Transfer scones to a wire rack to completely cool before glazing.

MAKE GLAZE:

In a small bowl, stir the powdered sugar, milk, and vanilla until smooth. Drizzle over the scones and let set for 5 minutes before serving.

SCONES

½ cup rye flour

½ cup all-purpose flour

2 teaspoons baking powder

¼ teaspoon baking soda

¼ teaspoon cinnamon

¼ teaspoon salt

3 tablespoons vegan unsalted butter, cold and cubed

3 tablespoons dark raisins

¼ cup almond milk

1 tablespoon + 1 teaspoon applesauce

1 tablespoon maple syrup

1 teaspoon apple cider vinegar

GLAZE

2 tablespoons powdered sugar

¼ teaspoon almond milk

¼ teaspoon vanilla extract

PRUNE MUFFINS

YIELD: 4 MUFFINS

INGREDIENTS

¼ cup almond milk

1½ teaspoons apple cider vinegar

⅓ cup all-purpose flour

¼ cup whole wheat flour

⅓ cup chopped prunes

¼ cup sugar

2 tablespoons + 1 teaspoon oats, divided

1¾ teaspoons baking powder

1 teaspoon cinnamon

¼ teaspoon baking soda

⅛ teaspoon salt

3 tablespoons olive oil

1 tablespoon water

½ teaspoon vanilla extract

1 tablespoon chopped pecans

Healthy never tasted so good! These fiber-rich prune muffins are nutritious and filling. They're easy to make with basic pantry ingredients and bake up quickly in the oven. Moist and flavorful, these muffins are always a huge hit.

DIRECTIONS

Preheat oven to 400°F. Line a muffin tray with 4 liners.

In a medium bowl, combine the almond milk and vinegar. Set aside to curdle.

In another medium bowl, add the flours. Set aside 1 tablespoon chopped prunes for garnish and add the remaining to the bowl along with the sugar, 2 tablespoons oats, baking powder, cinnamon, baking soda, and salt. Stir to combine and set aside.

Add the olive oil, water, and vanilla to the curdled milk and stir well. Briskly fold in the dry ingredients half at a time and mix until just combined. Portion the batter between the muffin liners. Garnish with the chopped pecans and remaining prunes and oats.

Bake for 13 minutes or until the centers bounce back when gently pressed. Let cool for at least 10 minutes before serving.

ROSEMARY RYE CRACKERS

YIELD: ABOUT 25 CRACKERS

These light, crispy rosemary rye crackers are tasteful on their own, or alongside dips. I love baking with rye flour whenever possible. It contributes robust, complex flavor to baked goods—in addition to fiber and nutrients.

DIRECTIONS

Preheat oven to 425°F. Lightly grease a baking tray with olive oil and set it aside.

In a large bowl, combine the flours, rosemary, and salt. Make a well in the center and add the water and 2 tablespoons olive oil. Use a spatula or a bowl scraper to mix the dough until combined, then switch to your hands and knead until smooth. Cover bowl with a dish towel and let the dough rest for 5 minutes.

Divide the dough in half. Roll one piece between your palms to form a small cylinder and place it on a clean surface. Roll the dough into a rough 14×5–inch rectangle and lay it on the bottom half of the prepared baking tray. Roll out the remaining piece of dough and lay it on the top half of the baking tray.

Use a pizza cutter to cut (score) the dough into desired shapes. Use a fork to poke holes in each cracker. Lightly brush the tops with olive oil. Bake for 5 minutes, rotate tray, and bake 5 minutes more. Remove the crackers that are golden brown (the ones along the edges) and continue baking the remaining crackers for 3 to 4 more minutes. Once completely cool, separate the crackers and store in an airtight container.

INGREDIENTS

olive oil for brushing
½ cup all-purpose flour
⅓ cup rye flour
½ teaspoon finely
   chopped rosemary
¼ teaspoon salt
6 tablespoons water
2 tablespoons olive oil

SEEDED WHOLE WHEAT BREAD

YIELD: 1 (9×5×3-INCH) LOAF

INGREDIENTS

1¼ cups almond milk, warmed (110°F)

2 tablespoons brown sugar

1 tablespoon molasses

1 (¼-ounce) packet active dry yeast

3 cups whole wheat flour, plus more for rolling

3 tablespoons unsalted vegan butter, melted

1 teaspoon salt

1 tablespoon sesame seeds

1 tablespoon sunflower seeds

1 tablespoon flax seeds

water for brushing

This whole wheat loaf is my go-to bread for sandwiches and toast. It's packed with protein, fiber, omega-3 and -6, vitamins, and minerals. Baked with flax, sesame, and sunflower seeds, this bread is hearty and healthy.

FIRST RISE

In an electric mixer bowl, whisk together the almond milk, brown sugar, molasses, and yeast. Let sit for 5 minutes to activate yeast.

Add the flour, butter, and salt to the yeast mixture. Attach the dough hook and mix on low speed for 1 minute. Increase speed to medium and mix for 3 minutes to develop the gluten. Transfer dough to a lightly greased bowl, and cover with a dish towel. Let rise in a warm place until doubled in size, about 45 minutes.

SECOND RISE

Combine the sesame, sunflower, and flax seeds on a large plate (oval works best). Grease a 9×5×3-inch loaf pan and set aside.

Punch down the dough, and transfer to a lightly floured surface. Roll the dough to an approximate 8×15–inch rectangle. Starting at one of the short sides, tightly roll up the dough into a log. Lightly brush the dough with water and roll it in the seed mixture to coat all over. Place the dough into the prepared pan, lightly brush the top with water, and cover with a dish towel. Let sit in a warm place until the dough rises 1 inch above the rim, about 1 hour. During the last 30 minutes of the rise, preheat oven to 375°F and adjust the oven rack to a lower position.

BAKE BREAD:

Bake for 20 minutes. Loosely tent with aluminum foil and bake 8 minutes more until loaf sounds hollow when tapped or the center reaches 190°F. Let cool for 15 minutes in pan before inverting onto a wire rack. Cool completely before slicing.

GARLIC NAANS

OIL-FREE | YIELD: 2 NAANS

This garlic naan is soft and squishy with a wonderfully chewy texture. It's cooked in a cast-iron pan—my affordable alternative to a tandoor. Enjoy this naan alone or as a sandwich (see Eggplant Wrap on page 87).

FIRST RISE

Warm the almond milk in the microwave to 110°F. Whisk in the sugar and yeast. Set aside until foamy, about 5 minutes.

In a large bowl, whisk together the flour, garlic, and salt. Pour in the yeast mixture. Mix with a spatula until dough comes together and no trace of flour remains. Transfer the dough to a small, lightly greased bowl. Cover with a dish towel and let rise for 45 minutes.

COOK NAANS:

Warm a large cast-iron pan over medium-high heat. Invert the dough onto a clean counter and divide the dough in half. Use your fingers to gently pat down and stretch each piece into a ¼-inch-thick rectangular oval. Lift the dough occasionally to prevent sticking. Place one naan in the pan and cook until top is puffy and bottom is golden brown, about 2 minutes. Flip and continue cooking for 1 to 2 minutes until cooked through. Repeat this step with second naan. Garnish naans with chopped cilantro and serve warm.

INGREDIENTS

½ cup almond milk
2 teaspoons sugar
1 teaspoon active dry yeast
1¼ cups all-purpose flour
1 garlic clove, minced
¼ teaspoon salt
chopped cilantro for garnish

WHOLESOME BREAKFASTS

Breakfast can be daunting and perplexing for those new to plant-based eating. Traditional breakfast fare consists largely of animal products, leaving many feeling stuck with just fruit and grains. Thankfully, plant-ifying breakfast is totally doable and delicious. The wholesome morning meals in this chapter will help you feel energized, nourished, and ready to take on any task.

ONE-BOWL BREAKFAST COOKIES

YIELD: 2 COOKIES

Cookies for breakfast? Yes, please! These healthy one-bowl morning cookies are simple to make and taste incredible. They're moist, chewy, and packed with good-for-you ingredients.

DIRECTIONS

Preheat oven to 350°F. Line a baking tray with parchment and set aside.

In a large bowl, stir together the oats, brown sugar, cranberries, oil, coconut, maple syrup, water, and agave. Let mixture sit for 5 minutes.

Add the flour, pecans, hemp seeds, baking soda, baking powder, cinnamon, and salt and stir until all ingredients are incorporated (mixture will be slightly crumbly). Divide the dough in half and shape into two balls. Place on the prepared tray and flatten to ¾ of an inch thick. Bake for 11 to 12 minutes until lightly browned and centers are just set. Do not overbake.

INGREDIENTS

6 tablespoons oats

3 tablespoons brown sugar

2 tablespoons dried cranberries

2 tablespoons olive oil

1 tablespoon unsweetened shredded coconut

1 tablespoon maple syrup

1½ teaspoons water

1 teaspoon agave nectar

⅓ cup all-purpose flour

2 tablespoons chopped pecans

½ teaspoon hemp seeds

⅛ teaspoon baking soda

⅛ teaspoon baking powder

⅛ teaspoon cinnamon

⅛ teaspoon salt

BUTTER & BERRY TOAST

OIL-FREE | YIELD: 2 SERVINGS

INGREDIENTS

4 slices of whole grain
   bread (or 2 bagels)
1 cup nut or seed butter
2 cups mixed berries or
   fruit
maple syrup for drizzling
optional garnishes: nuts,
   seeds, granola

Don't be fooled by the short list of ingredients here. These breakfast toasts are hearty enough to satisfy the most serious morning hunger pangs. Choose from nut butters like cashew, almond, and peanut. Or, use seed butters like sunflower or pumpkin. I like to mix peanut, cashew, and sunflower butters—it's a full-flavored combo!

DIRECTIONS

Toast the bread slices. Spread ¼ cup of butter on top of each slice. Cover with berries and drizzle with maple syrup. Top with optional garnishes, if desired.

AVOCADO TOAST

OIL-FREE | YIELD: 2 SERVINGS

My goal for this dish was to turn basic avocado toast into something heartier and tastier. The result was protein-packed scallion tofu "eggs" piled high atop avocado and covered with pickled red onions, greens, cucumber, and sriracha. Give this recipe a try; it's pretty darn delicious!

MAKE PICKLED ONIONS:
In a small bowl, warm the water in the microwave. Add the sugar and salt and stir to dissolve. Add the vinegar and submerge the sliced onions. Set aside to pickle.

MAKE TOFU "EGGS":
Wrap the tofu in paper towels and let sit for 5 minutes to dry.

Chop the scallions into ¼-inch pieces and place them in a medium bowl. Add the remaining ingredients including the tofu. Use a fork to break up the tofu and mix until all the ingredients are incorporated.

ASSEMBLE TOAST:
Crisp the bread in a toaster. Arrange avocado slices on each toast. Top with the tofu eggs, pickled red onions, greens, cucumber slices, and drops of sriracha.

PICKLED ONIONS
¼ cup water
1 tablespoon sugar
½ teaspoon salt
¼ cup white vinegar
¼ cup thinly sliced red onion

TOFU "EGGS"
7 ounces soft tofu
2 scallions
1 tablespoon nutritional yeast
1 tablespoon tahini
1 teaspoon white wine vinegar
1 teaspoon miso
½ teaspoon garlic powder
¼ teaspoon chili powder
⅛ teaspoon salt

TOAST
2–4 slices of sturdy whole grain bread
1 medium ripe avocado, sliced
handful of mixed greens
1 Persian cucumber, thinly sliced
sriracha to taste

NUT & SEED GRANOLA

GLUTEN-FREE | OIL-FREE | YIELD: ABOUT 4 CUPS

INGREDIENTS

1½ cups unsweetened
   shredded coconut
¼ cup raw sunflower
   seeds
¼ cup raw sesame seeds
¾ cup raw almonds
½ cup raw pepitas
¼ cup raw walnuts
⅓ cup maple syrup
¾ teaspoon cinnamon
⅛ teaspoon salt

This grain-free granola is a staple in our home. It's delicate, crisp, and full of healthy fats thanks to a variety of nuts and seeds. Enjoy this nutritious granola with dairy-free milk, sprinkled over soy yogurt, or by the handful!

DIRECTIONS

Preheat oven to 300°F. Line a baking tray with parchment and set aside.

Place the coconut, sunflower seeds, and sesame seeds in a large bowl and set aside. Working in batches, use a food processor to chop the almonds, pepitas, and walnuts into small pieces. Add the chopped nuts to the large bowl, and mix together well.

In a small bowl, stir the maple syrup, cinnamon, and salt. Pour over the coconut mixture, and stir until incorporated. Spread evenly on the prepared tray.

Bake for 20 minutes. Stir and bake 8 to 10 minutes more until evenly golden brown. Cool completely on the tray and store in an airtight container for up to 2 weeks.

APPLE & FIG OATMEAL

GLUTEN-FREE | OIL-FREE | YIELD: 2 SERVINGS

This chunky oatmeal is a family favorite, especially during cooler months. Sweetened with cinnamon and maple syrup and packed with chewy figs, tender apples, and crunchy walnuts, this wholesome breakfast will keep you satiated for hours.

DIRECTIONS

Add walnuts to a small pan over medium heat. Toast for 4 to 5 minutes, stirring frequently. Transfer to a plate and set aside.

In a small nonstick pot, add the chopped apples, 1 tablespoon maple syrup, cinnamon, and salt. Cook the apples over medium heat for 2 to 3 minutes, stirring occasionally, until the apples have slightly softened. Add 1½ cups warm water and bring to a boil. Stir in the oats. Cook, stirring occasionally, for 10 minutes at a low boil until thickened and most of the water has been absorbed. Stir in the figs, and cook 1 minute more.

Transfer oatmeal to two bowls. Garnish with the toasted walnuts and a drizzle of maple syrup.

INGREDIENTS

¼ cup raw walnut pieces

1 cup chopped apples

1 tablespoon maple syrup, plus more for drizzling

½ teaspoon cinnamon

pinch of salt

1½ cups warm water

1 cup oats

3 dried figs, cut into bite-sized pieces

APPLE OATCAKES

GLUTEN-FREE | OIL-FREE | YIELD: 2 SERVINGS
(8 OATCAKES)

FLAX EGG
3 tablespoons warm water
1 tablespoon flaxseed meal

OATCAKES
1½ cups oats
¼ cup almond flour, sifted
1 tablespoon baking powder
½ teaspoon cinnamon
¾ cup almond milk
¼ cup coconut milk
¼ cup unsweetened applesauce
2 teaspoons molasses
1 small apple, cut into bite-sized pieces
maple syrup for serving

These tender gluten-free oatcakes are made with oats, applesauce, and molasses. The earthy oatcakes pair wonderfully with the juicy crunch of apples and sweet maple syrup.

MAKE FLAX EGG:
In a small bowl, combine the water and flaxseed meal. Let sit for 5 minutes to thicken.

MAKE OATCAKES:
In a food processor, add the oats and blend until finely ground. Transfer to a large bowl and add the almond flour, baking powder, and cinnamon. In a liquid measure, stir the milks, applesauce, and molasses until combined. Add the wet ingredients—including the flax egg—to the dry ingredients and whisk until smooth. Let the batter sit for 10 minutes to thicken while you warm a nonstick griddle over medium-low heat.

Portion ⅓ cup of batter onto the griddle. Cook for 4 to 5 minutes until batter slightly puffs and edges set by about ½ inch. Flip and cook 30 to 40 seconds. Serve oatcakes warm with chopped apples and maple syrup.

BLACKBERRY THYME FRENCH TOAST

YIELD: 2 SERVINGS

This quick and easy French toast is tastier than any egg-based version. Thick slices of rustic bread are dipped in a batter flavored with cinnamon, vanilla, and thyme, cooked to golden perfection, and served with juicy, sweet blackberries.

DIRECTIONS

In a small pot, whisk the almond milk, powdered sugar, cinnamon, vanilla, and thyme. Bring to a simmer over medium heat. Cover, turn off heat, and let steep 5 minutes. Discard thyme sprigs.

Working one at a time, dip the bread slices in the batter for a few seconds per side and arrange them on a plate. Warm a large skillet over medium heat. Add the butter and swirl to coat the pan. Cook the bread slices until golden brown, about 2 to 3 minutes per side. Serve with blackberries and maple syrup.

INGREDIENTS

½ cup almond milk

1 teaspoon powdered sugar

⅛ teaspoon cinnamon

⅛ teaspoon vanilla extract

1–2 sprigs thyme

4 (1-inch-thick) slices whole grain rustic bread

1 tablespoon vegan unsalted butter

⅓ cup blackberries

maple syrup for serving

BITTER GREENS SALAD

GLUTEN-FREE | YIELD: 2 SERVINGS

Bitter and spicy dandelion and radicchio are perfectly balanced by sweet, roasted beets and a citrusy carrot ginger dressing. The combination of bright, distinct flavors in this salad awakens the palate and completely satisfies.

ROAST BEETS:
Preheat oven to 400°F. Wrap the beets in foil. Roast for 1 hour or until a paring knife is easily inserted into the flesh. Remove the skin, cut into slices or wedges, and set them aside.

MAKE CARROT GINGER DRESSING:
Add all ingredients to a small food processor. Mix on high until smooth. Season with pepper to taste.

ASSEMBLE SALAD:
Divide the dandelion greens and radicchio between two salad bowls. Top with the roasted beets and serve with the carrot ginger dressing.

BEETS
12 ounces trimmed golden beets (about 3 medium)

CARROT GINGER DRESSING
1 small carrot, chopped

1 small celery rib, chopped

1 garlic clove, chopped

1-inch strip of orange peel, finely chopped

¼ cup olive oil

2 tablespoons minced yellow onion

2 tablespoons rice vinegar

2 tablespoons silken tofu

1½ tablespoons chopped ginger

1½ teaspoons miso

1½ teaspoons sugar

pepper to taste

SALAD
4 cups chopped dandelion greens

2 cups chopped radicchio

WARM CAULIFLOWER SALAD

GLUTEN-FREE | YIELD: 2 SERVINGS

LEMON TAHINI DRESSING

1 garlic clove, pressed
2 tablespoons tahini
1 tablespoon water
1 teaspoon lemon juice
1 teaspoon olive oil
1 teaspoon apple cider
   vinegar
¼ teaspoon salt
pepper to taste

CROUTONS

¾ cup (½-inch-cubed)
   whole grain bread
1½ teaspoons extra-virgin
   olive oil
⅛ teaspoon pepper
⅛ teaspoon salt

SALAD

3 cups cauliflower florets
3 tablespoons +
   ½ teaspoon olive oil,
   divided
½ teaspoon garlic powder
¼ teaspoon cumin
¼ teaspoon + ⅛ teaspoon
   salt, divided
2 tablespoons cornstarch
4 ounces extra-firm tofu,
   frozen and thawed
5–6 deglet noor dates,
   sliced
4 cups arugula, lightly
   chopped

This nutrient-packed salad combines roasted, juicy cauliflower, peppery arugula, and crisp tofu all tossed in a creamy lemon tahini dressing. Homemade croutons and sweet, pan-fried dates add great flavor, texture, and crunch.

DIRECTIONS

Preheat oven to 350°F. Set aside a parchment-lined baking tray.

MAKE LEMON TAHINI DRESSING:

In a small bowl, whisk together all the ingredients until smooth. Set aside.

MAKE CROUTONS:

Place the bread cubes, olive oil, pepper, and salt on the parchment-lined baking tray. Toss to coat and spread out evenly. Bake for 10 minutes until golden and crisp. Transfer to a bowl and set aside. Discard parchment and increase oven temperature to 425°F.

MAKE SALAD:

In a large bowl, combine the cauliflower, 1 tablespoon olive oil, garlic powder, cumin, and ¼ teaspoon salt. Toss well and evenly spread out onto the baking tray. Roast for 20 minutes.

Meanwhile, stir together the cornstarch, 2 tablespoons olive oil, and ⅛ teaspoon salt in a small bowl. Squeeze out as much water from the tofu as possible. Cut the tofu into 8 cubes, add them to the slurry, and stir to coat. Warm a medium skillet over medium-low heat. Cook the tofu cubes until crisp, about 2 minutes per side. Transfer to a plate and set aside.

In a small skillet, warm ½ teaspoon olive oil over medium heat. Add the dates and cook, stirring, for 1 to 2 minutes until lightly browned. Transfer to a plate and set aside.

ASSEMBLE SALAD:

In a large bowl, combine the crisped tofu, roasted cauliflower, fried dates, croutons, and arugula. Drizzle the tahini dressing on top and toss to coat. Portion between two bowls and serve.

MEDITERRANEAN BROCCOLI SALAD

GLUTEN-FREE | YIELD: 2 SERVINGS

This Mediterranean broccoli salad is super easy to make and can be made up to 24 hours in advance. Tender broccoli florets combine with quinoa, chickpeas, roasted almonds, parsley, red onions, olives, and sun-dried tomatoes to make a healthy, protein-packed meal.

COOK QUINOA:
In a small pot, combine the water and quinoa. Bring to a simmer over medium heat and cook, covered, for 22 minutes or until all the water is absorbed. Keep covered and remove from heat.

BLANCH BROCCOLI:
Fill a large bowl with ice water and set aside. Fill a medium pot halfway with water and bring to a boil over high heat. Trim the broccoli crown and cut into small florets. Add to the boiling water and cook for 2 minutes. Drain and immediately plunge the florets in the ice bath. Swirl to cool and transfer to a colander to drain.

MAKE GREEK VINAIGRETTE:
In a large bowl, whisk together all the ingredients.

ASSEMBLE SALAD:
Add the parsley, chickpeas, almonds, onion, olives, tomatoes, quinoa, and broccoli to the dressing and stir to coat. Can be served immediately or stored in the refrigerator for up to 24 hours.

QUINOA
1 cup water
⅓ cup quinoa

BROCCOLI
1 (12–14-ounce) broccoli crown
water for blanching

GREEK VINAIGRETTE
2 garlic cloves, minced
¼ cup extra-virgin olive oil
2 tablespoons lemon juice
1 teaspoon dried oregano
½ teaspoon sugar
½ teaspoon salt
¼ teaspoon pepper

SALAD
1 cup chopped parsley
½ cup chickpeas, rinsed
½ cup roasted almonds, chopped
¼ cup thinly sliced red onion
¼ cup Kalamata olives, halved or whole
¼ cup finely chopped sun-dried tomatoes

HEARTY HANDHELDS

It's hard not to love handhelds. They're comfort-inducing, quick to make, and easy to eat without the need for utensils. They are a complete nutrition package in your hand—and at your fingertips. The best part? Handhelds are customizable in unlimited ways. *Don't like olives?* Leave them out. *Allergic to walnuts?* Use cashews instead. *Not a fan of rosemary?* Try thyme. *Don't care for baguettes (gasp)?* Stuff it in a pita. I hope you take these recipes and add your own creative flair. That's really what cooking is all about!

VEGGIE HUMMUS PITAS

YIELD: 2 SERVINGS (4 PITA HALVES)

Craving a fast, healthy meal? These tasty pita sandwiches are slathered with creamy hummus and stuffed with a tabouli-like salad of baby spinach, radishes, cucumbers, parsley, and tomatoes. A chia seed red wine vinaigrette adds a burst of flavor.

MAKE HUMMUS:

In a small pot, combine the chickpeas and baking soda and cover with water by 2 inches. Bring to a boil over high heat and cook for 20 minutes. Drain and rinse.

In a food processor, add the chickpeas and remaining hummus ingredients. Blend on high until smooth. Scrape down the bowl as needed. Transfer to a bowl and set aside.

MAKE VINAIGRETTE:

In a small bowl, stir together all the ingredients. Set aside for 5 minutes to slightly thicken.

MAKE SALAD:

In a large bowl, combine the spinach, parsley, tomatoes, avocado, cucumber, and radishes. Pour the vinaigrette on top and toss to coat.

ASSEMBLE PITAS:

Cut the pita rounds in half and split open. Spread hummus inside and stuff with salad. Serve immediately.

HUMMUS

1 cup chickpeas, rinsed
¼ teaspoon baking soda
water for boiling
2 garlic cloves, pressed
3 tablespoons tahini
2 tablespoons water
1 tablespoon extra-virgin olive oil
1 tablespoon lemon juice
¼ teaspoon salt
⅛ teaspoon ground cumin
⅛ teaspoon paprika

VINAIGRETTE

2 tablespoons red wine vinegar
½ teaspoon chia seeds
¼ teaspoon maple syrup
salt and pepper to taste

SALAD

2 cups finely chopped baby spinach
½ cup finely chopped parsley
½ cup grape tomatoes, halved lengthwise
1 small avocado, small-diced
1 Persian cucumber, small-diced
2 radishes, thinly sliced
2 whole wheat pita rounds

JACKFRUIT BURRITOS

YIELD: 2 BURRITOS

RICE
1 cup water
½ teaspoon olive oil
pinch of salt
½ cup long-grain brown rice

JACKFRUIT
1 (14.1-ounce) can organic young green jackfruit, drained and rinsed
1 garlic clove, chopped
¼ cup chipotle chilis in adobe sauce
2 tablespoons orange juice
1 tablespoon chopped dill
1 tablespoon olive oil
1 tablespoon apple cider vinegar
⅛ teaspoon cumin
salt and pepper to taste

BURRITO
2 large (12-inch) flour tortillas
⅔ cup refried beans (black or traditional)
½ cup diced red onion
¼ cup chopped cilantro
1 small avocado, pitted and sliced

This satisfying burrito is smoky and tangy. Shredded jackfruit is baked in a fiery chipotle marinade and rolled up in a giant tortilla stuffed with brown rice, red onion, and avocado. If you have cooked rice ready to go, you'll need 2 cups.

DIRECTIONS
Preheat oven to 400°F and set aside a parchment-lined baking tray.

MAKE RICE:
In a small pot, bring water, oil, and salt to a boil over high heat. Stir in the brown rice and reduce to a simmer. Cover and cook for 30 minutes. Remove pot from heat and let sit 10 minutes before fluffing. Keep covered and set aside.

COOK JACKFRUIT:
In a large bowl, shred the jackfruit with your hands and set aside.

In a food processor, add the garlic, chilis, orange juice, dill, oil, vinegar, and cumin. Blend until smooth and season with salt and pepper. Pour over the jackfruit and stir to coat. Spread evenly onto the prepared tray and bake for 20 minutes. Stir and bake 8 minutes more.

ASSEMBLE BURRITO:
Lay the tortillas on a clean surface. Spread the beans on the bottom third of each tortilla, leaving a 1-inch border. Top with brown rice, jackfruit, red onion, cilantro, and avocado. Roll up, burrito-style.

Warm a cast-iron pan over medium heat. Crisp the burritos all over, about 2 to 3 minutes per side. Slice in half, if desired, and serve.

MUSHROOM PÂTÉ EN BAGUETTES

YIELD: 2 SANDWICHES

Classic French pâté sandwiches are divine. This vegan version is no exception. Earthy mushrooms cooked with shallots, rosemary, garlic, and parsley are blended with lentils and spread on a warm, crusty baguette. You will absolutely love how easy these are to make.

MAKE PÂTÉ:

In a large skillet, warm the olive oil over medium-high heat. Add ¼ cup shallots and cook until translucent, about 2 minutes. Add the mushrooms, garlic, parsley, rosemary, salt, and pepper. Cook until tender and any liquid released from the mushrooms has evaporated, about 8 to 10 minutes. Transfer to a food processor. Add the lentils and blend on high until smooth. Scrape bowl as needed. (If desired, you can chill the pâté in the refrigerator until cool.)

ASSEMBLE SANDWICH:

Preheat oven to 350°F. Slice baguette in half lengthwise. Place directly on oven rack and bake 5 minutes until lightly toasted. Spread a thin layer of Dijon mustard on the top. Spread the pâté on the bottom and cover with mixed greens, olives, and the remaining sliced shallots. Cover with top baguette, cut in half on the diagonal, and serve.

PÂTÉ

2 teaspoons olive oil
½ cup thinly sliced shallots, divided
8 ounces cremini mushrooms, chopped
1 garlic clove, minced
¼ cup chopped parsley
1 teaspoon finely chopped rosemary
¼ teaspoon salt
pinch of pepper
½ cup canned brown lentils*, drained and rinsed

SANDWICH

1 medium baguette
Dijon mustard
1 cup mixed greens
¼ cup sliced marinated olives (store-bought or recipe on page 182)

*If starting with raw lentils, cook scant ¼ cup in boiling water for 20 minutes to yield ½ cup cooked lentils.

TAHINI MUSTARD SAUCE

2 teaspoons tahini

1 teaspoon white wine vinegar

1 teaspoon maple syrup

1 teaspoon Dijon mustard

BURGERS

1½ tablespoons warm water

1½ teaspoons flaxseed meal

½ cup oats

4 ounces cremini mushrooms

1 teaspoon olive oil

1 garlic clove, minced

¼ teaspoon smoked paprika

¼ teaspoon chili powder

½ teaspoon vegan Worcestershire

½ cup canned brown lentils*, drained and rinsed

¼ teaspoon salt

⅛ teaspoon pepper

2 slices vegan cheddar-style cheese

2 whole wheat burger buns

red onion, tomatoes, clover-alfalfa sprouts for garnish

*If starting with raw lentils, cook scant ¼ cup in boiling water for 20 minutes to yield ½ cup cooked lentils.

VEGGIE BURGERS

YIELD: 2 BURGERS

There's nothing more disappointing than a veggie patty that falls apart at first bite. Well, friends, this veggie burger will have you cheering with satisfaction. Mushrooms, lentils, and oats combine to give these patties great texture, and a blend of vegan Worcestershire, smoked paprika, and chili powder create an umami-packed burger that's truly the best I've ever had.

DIRECTIONS

Preheat oven to 400°F. Line a baking tray with parchment and set aside.

MAKE TAHINI MUSTARD SAUCE:

In a small bowl, stir together all the ingredients and set aside.

MAKE BURGERS:

In a small bowl, combine the water and flaxseed meal. Set aside to thicken.

Add ½ cup oats to a food processor and pulse until pulverized. Transfer to a large bowl and set aside.

Add the mushrooms to the processor and pulse until finely chopped. In a small skillet, warm 1 teaspoon olive oil over medium heat. Add the mushrooms and cook until all the water released from the mushrooms evaporates, about 7 minutes. Stir in the garlic, paprika, and chili powder and cook for one minute. Stir in the Worcestershire and cook for 10 seconds.

Transfer mushrooms to the large bowl (with the oats). Add the flax egg, lentils, salt, and pepper and mix with your hands until combined. Form two ½-inch-thick patties, and place on the prepared tray.

Bake for 15 minutes, flip, top with the cheese, and bake 5 minutes more. Transfer patties to the bun bottoms and garnish with the tahini mustard, red onions, tomatoes, and sprouts. Cover with tops and serve immediately.

EGGPLANT WRAPS

YIELD: 2 SERVINGS

Roasting is my favorite way to cook eggplant—the high heat caramelizes the skin and gives the flesh a smooth, luscious texture. In this hearty handheld, roasted eggplant is layered with greens, red onions, cilantro, and a creamy tahini ginger sauce, all wrapped in homemade garlic naan. The flavors are magnificent.

DIRECTIONS
Preheat oven to 450°F. Set aside a baking tray.

MAKE GARLIC NAAN:
Begin making the Garlic Naan recipe on page 47. While the dough rises, make the tahini ginger sauce and filling.

MAKE TAHINI GINGER SAUCE:
In a small bowl, stir all the ingredients together until combined and set aside. (Sauce will thicken as it sits.)

MAKE FILLING:
Cut the eggplant into 1-inch-thick slices and place them in a large bowl. Toss with olive oil and season with salt and pepper. Lay the slices in an even layer on the baking tray. Roast for 20 minutes. Flip the eggplant slices and roast 5 minutes more until caramelized and tender. Remove tray from oven and set aside.

FINISH MAKING NAAN:
Cook the garlic naan according to the recipe.

ASSEMBLE WRAP:
Spread the tahini sauce on the naans. On one half of each naan, layer the mixed greens, red onions, cilantro, and eggplant slices. Fold to close and serve.

GARLIC NAAN
recipe on page 47

TAHINI GINGER SAUCE
2 tablespoons tahini
2 teaspoons maple syrup
2 teaspoons lemon juice
1½ teaspoons water
1 teaspoon grated ginger
½ teaspoon miso

FILLING
1 Chinese eggplant
   (about 8 ounces)
2 tablespoons olive oil
salt and pepper to taste
1 cup mixed greens
½ cup sliced red onions
½ cup cilantro, lightly
   packed

SWEET POTATO TACOS

GLUTEN-FREE | YIELD: 2 SERVINGS

SLAW

1 garlic clove, pressed

1½ tablespoons lime juice

1½ tablespoons chopped chipotle chilis in adobe sauce

1 tablespoon chopped cilantro

2 teaspoons maple syrup

⅛ teaspoon salt

2 cups thinly shredded cabbage (green or red)

FILLING

1 sweet potato (about 14 ounces)

½ cup frozen corn kernels

2 tablespoons olive oil

¼ teaspoon garlic powder

¼ teaspoon dried oregano

⅛ teaspoon salt

⅛ teaspoon pepper

TACOS

4–6 small corn tortillas

1 small avocado, sliced

When you're looking for a quick and tasty dinner, these boldly flavored tacos are a terrific choice. Creamy roasted sweet potato, caramelized bits of corn, and a tangy, chipotle slaw nestled in warm corn tortillas make these tacos unforgettable.

DIRECTIONS

Preheat the oven to 400°F. Set aside a large baking tray.

MAKE SLAW:

In a medium bowl, whisk the first 6 ingredients. Mix in the shredded cabbage. Cover and set aside.

MAKE FILLING:

Peel and cut the potato into ½-inch cubes. Transfer them to a large bowl and toss with the corn, olive oil, garlic powder, oregano, salt, and pepper. Spread onto the baking tray in an even layer and roast for 30 minutes.

ASSEMBLE TACOS:

Warm tortillas over a gas flame. Fill with the roasted vegetables, cabbage slaw, and slices of avocado and serve.

SWEET POTATO SANDWICHES

YIELD: 2 SANDWICHES

I had my first sweet potato sandwich years ago while on a cross-country road trip, and I've been hooked on them ever since. In this version, fresh dill adds a clean, bright taste to a buttery avocado mash that's paired with creamy roasted sweet potatoes and crunchy veggies.

ROAST SWEET POTATOES:

Preheat oven to 400°F. Line a baking tray with parchment and set aside.

Peel the sweet potato and cut it into ¼-inch-thick slices. Place in a large bowl and toss with the olive oil, garlic powder, and salt. Arrange in a single layer on the prepared baking tray and roast for 20 minutes. Set aside.

MAKE DILL AVOCADO MASH:

In a medium bowl, add the avocado flesh, dill, garlic, vinegar, and salt. Use the back of a fork to mash the mixture until combined.

ASSEMBLE SANDWICH:

Spread the avocado mash onto two slices of bread. Top with the roasted sweet potatoes, cucumber slices, rings of red onion, and spinach. Cover with remaining bread and serve.

SWEET POTATO
1 sweet potato
   (12–14 ounces)
1 tablespoon olive oil
¼ teaspoon garlic powder
¼ teaspoon salt

DILL AVOCADO MASH
1 large ripe avocado,
   pitted and halved
¼ cup chopped dill
1 garlic clove, minced
½ teaspoon apple cider
   vinegar
¼ teaspoon salt

SANDWICH
4 slices whole grain
   bread
1 small Persian cucumber,
   thinly sliced
2 rings of red onion
handful of baby spinach

EMPANADAS

YIELD: 2 SERVINGS (5 TO 6 EMPANADAS)

DOUGH
1¼ cups all-purpose flour

¼ cup whole wheat flour

¾ teaspoon baking powder

½ teaspoon salt

6 tablespoons vegan unsalted butter, cold and cubed

6–7 tablespoons ice water

FILLING
2 Portobello mushrooms

1 (8-ounce) Yukon gold potato

2 teaspoons olive oil

½ cup small-diced yellow onion

2 garlic cloves, minced

2 tablespoons brandy

½ teaspoon salt

⅛ teaspoon pepper

1 cup coconut milk

¼ cup chopped parsley

You and yours will love these tender, flaky empanadas filled with a creamy mix of Portobello mushroom, potato, and onion. To sneak in some nutrition, I use whole wheat flour in the crust, top them with seeds, and bake—instead of fry—them.

MAKE DOUGH:

In a large bowl, combine the flours, baking powder, and salt. Add the butter and use a pastry cutter to break it down into pea size. Sprinkle 6 tablespoons ice water on top and mix with your hands until the dough comes together. Add more water if needed. Shape into a disc, wrap with plastic, and chill in the refrigerator while you make the filling.

MAKE FILLING:

Remove the gills and stems from the mushrooms. Cut into ½-inch cubes and set aside. Peel potato if desired. Cut into ¼-inch-thick, bite-sized pieces and set aside.

In a large skillet, warm 2 teaspoons olive oil over medium heat. Add the onions and garlic. Cook, stirring occasionally, for 3 minutes until the onions are tender and lightly browned. Stir in the mushrooms and cook for 5 minutes until caramelized. Deglaze the pan with 2 tablespoons brandy and cook until evaporated. Add the potatoes, salt, and pepper and cook for one minute. Stir in the coconut milk. Cover and cook, stirring occasionally, at a medium-low boil for 13 to 15 minutes until potatoes are tender and sauce has thickened. Stir in the parsley, transfer mixture to a bowl, and place in the refrigerator to cool.

(*Ingredients and Directions continued on 94*)

GARNISH

1 teaspoon almond milk

⅛ teaspoon turmeric

½–1 teaspoon raw seeds
 (e.g., sesame, pepitas,
 sunflower)

2 teaspoons maple syrup

ASSEMBLE EMPANADAS:

Preheat oven to 400°F. Line a baking tray with parchment.

On a lightly floured surface, roll the dough to an ⅛-inch thickness. Cut out five to six (6-inch) circles from the dough, rerolling the scraps as needed, and place them on the prepared tray. Working one at a time, spoon about ⅓ cup of filling onto one side of each round, leaving a ½-inch border. Moisten the edges with water and fold to close. Use a fork to decoratively seal the edges.

GARNISH AND BAKE EMPANADAS:

In a small bowl, combine the almond milk and turmeric. Brush the tops of the empanadas and sprinkle seeds on top. Bake for 20 minutes. Remove tray from oven and brush the tops with maple syrup. Return to oven and bake 10 minutes more. Serve warm.

VEGETABLE SPRING ROLLS

GLUTEN-FREE | YIELD: 2 SERVINGS (ABOUT 10 ROLLS)

These fresh Vietnamese spring rolls are made with lettuce, sprouts, red bell peppers, cucumber, carrot, and herbs wrapped in rice paper. They're delightfully crunchy and served with a flavorful black sesame seed peanut sauce. Prepping the vegetables first makes assembling these rolls a breeze.

MAKE PEANUT SAUCE:

In a food processor, add the first nine ingredients. Blend until combined, scraping the bowl down as needed. Add ¼ cup of water a little at a time, mixing well after each addition. Set aside.

PREP ROLLS:

Set aside a large tray or plate. Cut off the bottom of the romaine lettuce so the leaves separate. Cut the leaves from the stalks (you can keep the very tiny inside leaves intact). Place the leaves on the tray. Cut the stalks into small, bite-sized pieces and transfer to the tray.

Core the bell pepper and cut into long, thin strips. Place on the tray. Cut the carrot into 2- to 3-inch-long matchsticks and place them on the tray. Cut the cucumbers into 2- to 3-inch-long matchsticks and place them on the tray. Place the mixed herbs on the tray. Have the package of sprouts nearby.

ASSEMBLE ROLLS:

Fill a large, shallow dish with lukewarm water. Dip one rice paper in the water for 1 to 2 seconds and lay it on a cutting board. On the bottom ⅓ of the paper (closest to you), lay a few torn pieces of romaine leaves in the middle so they cover about 4 inches. Top the leaves with some chopped romaine stalk, sprouts, and cucumbers. About half an inch in front of the filling, lay some bell pepper and carrots. About half an inch in front of that, lay a line

(Continued)

PEANUT SAUCE

2 garlic cloves, peeled
½ cup roasted, salted peanuts
2 tablespoons tahini
2 tablespoons sesame oil
2 tablespoons maple syrup
2 tablespoons hoisin sauce
2 teaspoons miso
2 teaspoons lemon juice
1 teaspoon black sesame seeds
¼ cup water for thinning

ROLLS

1 small romaine lettuce
1 small red bell pepper
1 large carrot
2 Persian cucumbers
1 cup fresh mixed herbs (mint, basil, cilantro)
1 (3-ounce) package sprouts (I like clover-broccoli blend)
lukewarm water
10 rice papers (22cm)

of herbs. Pick up the edge closest to you. Wrap and roll the rice paper completely around the lettuce mixture. Fold in the left and right sides. Continue rolling all the way up like a burrito. Repeat this step with the remaining rice papers.

SERVE ROLLS:

If desired, cut the rolls in half. Serve the spring rolls with the peanut sauce. These rolls are best eaten the day they're made.

HOW TO BUILD A PLANT-BASED BOWL

There is no one right way to build a plant-based bowl. They're entirely customizable, experimental, and a great way to use up what's in your refrigerator. But if you need a place to start, the guide below will help you put together a good combination of greens, carb, protein, and vegetable topped with sauce and crunch.

GREENS (1 cup)	CARB (½ cup)	PROTEIN (½–1 cup)	VEGETABLE (1 cup)	SAUCE (1–2 tablespoons)	TOPPING (1–2 tablespoons)
Spinach	Rice	Beans	Asparagus	Miso Dressing	Nori
Chard	Quinoa	Pulses	Broccoli	Peanut Sauce	Seeds
Beet	Farro	Edamame	Brussels Sprouts	Tomatillo Sauce	Avocado
Arugula	Barley	Chickpeas	Cabbage	Salsa	Kimchi
Kale	Millet	Lentils	Carrots	Hot Sauce	Scallions
Lettuce	Sorghum	Tofu	Cauliflower	Vinaigrettes	Sprouts
Watercress	Wheat Berries	Tempeh	Cucumber	Dairy-free Yogurt	Olives
	Potatoes		Eggplant	Tahini	Herbs
	Plantains		Green Beans	Citrus Dressing	Coconut
	Winter Squash		Mushrooms		
	Root Vegetables		Onions		
	Beets		Peppers		
	Amaranth		Radishes		
	Peas		Squash		
	Corn		Sweet Potatoes		
	Pasta		Tomatoes		

HEALTHY ENTRÉES

This chapter has healthy, plant-based entrées sure to satisfy any craving. I've included my favorite pasta dishes, some veggie-heavy standouts, a vibrant grain bowl, a killer curry, a couple classic Southern dishes, and more!

PEANUT NOODLES WITH BAKED SESAME TOFU

YIELD: 2 SERVINGS

A quick and easy noodle dish you can make—stress free! Slurpy noodles are coated in a yummy peanut sauce and served with baked sesame tofu, scallions, and crunchy peanuts.

DIRECTIONS
Preheat oven to 400°F. Line a baking sheet with parchment and set aside.

MAKE PEANUT SAUCE:
In a small bowl, add the first seven ingredients. Warm 10 seconds in the microwave and whisk until combined. Thin with 3 tablespoons water. Set aside.

BAKE SESAME TOFU:
In a shallow bowl or large plate, stir together the soy sauce, sesame oil, and miso until combined. Cut the tofu into ½-inch-thick squares and coat with the sauce on all sides. Marinate for 10 minutes, flipping once halfway. Lay the tofu on the prepared baking tray, sprinkle sesame seeds on top, and bake for 25 minutes.

COOK NOODLES:
Fill a medium pot with lightly salted water and bring to a boil over high heat. Add the noodles and cook according to package directions. Drain and return noodles to pot. Pour ⅔ of the peanut sauce on top and stir to coat. Divide noodles between two bowls and top with the baked tofu. Garnish with scallions, peanuts, and cilantro, and serve with the remaining sauce.

PEANUT SAUCE
¼ cup coconut milk
¼ cup smooth peanut butter
2 tablespoons brown sugar
2 tablespoons less-sodium soy sauce
1 teaspoon sesame oil
½ teaspoon grated ginger
1 garlic clove, pressed
3 tablespoons water

SESAME TOFU
2 tablespoons less-sodium soy sauce
1 tablespoon sesame oil
1 teaspoon miso
7–8 ounces firm tofu, pressed
¼ teaspoon sesame seeds

NOODLES
lightly salted water for boiling
4 ounces whole grain spaghetti
1 scallion, thinly sliced
2 tablespoons finely chopped roasted, salted peanuts
2 tablespoons finely chopped cilantro

ROASTED EGGPLANT
WITH WALNUT PESTO PASTA

YIELD: 2 SERVINGS

PESTO

2 cups basil leaves, lightly
  packed
½ cup parsley leaves
  (stems okay), lightly
  packed
⅓ cup raw walnut halves,
  divided
1 tablespoon nutritional
  yeast
2 teaspoons lemon zest,
  plus more for garnish
1 teaspoon miso
1 teaspoon capers
1 garlic clove, peeled
3 tablespoons extra-
  virgin olive oil
salt and pepper to taste

EGGPLANT

1 medium (14-ounce)
  globe eggplant
3 tablespoons olive oil
salt and pepper to taste

PASTA

salted water for boiling
1½ cups whole grain rotini
  pasta
2 tablespoons Kalamata
  olives

This light, brightly flavored pasta will whisk you away to Italy with just one bite. The combination of lemon pesto, caramelized eggplant, briny olives, and crunchy walnuts is delightful.

MAKE PESTO:

Add the basil leaves, parsley, *half* the walnuts, nutritional yeast, lemon zest, miso, capers, and garlic to a food processor and blend until finely chopped. Add the olive oil 1 tablespoon at a time, pulsing after each addition. Season with salt and pepper and set aside.

ROAST EGGPLANT:

Preheat oven to 450°F and set aside a lightly greased baking tray.

Cut the eggplant into 1¼-inch-thick chunks. Place them in a large bowl, mix with 3 tablespoons olive oil, and season with salt and pepper. Evenly spread the eggplant onto the prepared tray. Roast 20 minutes, stir the eggplant, and roast 5 minutes more.

COOK PASTA:

While the eggplant roasts, cook the pasta in salted water according to package directions. *Reserve 2 tablespoons of pasta water before draining.* Transfer the drained pasta (no need to rinse) to a large bowl. Add the reserved pasta water 1 tablespoon at a time, stirring after each addition until absorbed. Add the pesto and stir to coat.

Portion the pasta onto two plates and top with the roasted eggplant. Garnish with olives, the remaining walnuts, and lemon zest before serving.

PASTA CACCIATORE

OIL-FREE | YIELD: 2 SERVINGS

This pasta cacciatore has all the wondrous flavors of the classic Italian dish—without meat. The spicy, chunky red sauce is packed with tomatoes, olives, mushrooms, red pepper, and onions.

DIRECTIONS

Warm a large nonstick pan over medium-low heat. Add the peppers, onions, mushrooms, garlic, oregano, salt, and chili flakes. Cook, stirring occasionally, for 5 minutes until slightly softened. If sticking occurs, reduce heat or splash vegetables with a little water. Add the red wine and boil until reduced by half, about 3 minutes. Stir in the tomatoes, broth, olives, parsley, tomato paste, and sugar. Add salt and pepper to taste. Cook at a low boil for 7 minutes or until desired consistency is reached. Cover and set aside.

Bring a medium pot of salted water to a boil over high heat. Cook the pasta according to package directions. Drain and add the pasta to the sauce and stir until evenly coated. Portion into two bowls and serve.

SAUCE
½ cup small-diced red bell pepper
½ cup small-diced onion
4 ounces cremini mushrooms, quartered
2 garlic cloves, minced
1 teaspoon dried oregano
½ teaspoon salt, plus more to taste
¼ teaspoon red chili flakes
½ cup red wine (I like cabernet)
1 cup canned crushed tomatoes
½ cup vegetable broth
¼ cup black or green olives, halved
¼ cup chopped parsley
1 tablespoon tomato paste
1 teaspoon sugar
pepper to taste

PASTA
salted water for boiling
4 ounces whole wheat penne

MUSHROOM RISOTTO

GLUTEN-FREE | YIELD: 2 SERVINGS

INGREDIENTS

2½ cups vegetable broth

2 teaspoons olive oil

4 ounces cremini mushrooms, cut into ¼-inch-thick slices

¼ cup chopped shallots

3 garlic cloves, minced, divided

8 ounces asparagus, trimmed and cut into 1-inch pieces

¼ teaspoon salt

2 tablespoons brandy

½ cup Arborio rice

¼ cup coconut milk

1 tablespoon nutritional yeast

This robust mushroom risotto is pure coziness in a bowl. Asparagus and mushrooms are sautéed with garlic and brandy. The rice is cooked separately until *al dente* and creamy. This risotto is the ultimate plant-based comfort food.

DIRECTIONS

In a small pot, warm the vegetable broth over low heat.

In a large skillet, warm 2 teaspoons olive oil over medium-high heat. Sauté the mushrooms, shallots, and *half* the garlic until tender, about 3 minutes. Add the asparagus and ¼ teaspoon salt. Sauté until stalks are just tender, but slightly crunchy, about 3 minutes. Add the brandy and cook for 5 to 10 seconds until evaporated. Transfer vegetables to a plate and set aside.

Wipe skillet with a paper towel and add the rice. Shaking the pan frequently, toast over medium heat until rice is lightly browned, about 3 minutes. Reduce heat to medium-low. Add the remaining chopped garlic, ½ cup of the warm broth, and slowly cook, stirring continuously, until liquid is completely absorbed. Continue adding and cooking the broth ½ cup at a time; this will take about 25 minutes total.

Remove skillet from heat and stir in the coconut milk, nutritional yeast, and sautéed vegetables. Serve immediately.

SPAGHETTI SQUASH SAUTÉ

GLUTEN-FREE | YIELD: 2 SERVINGS

I'm always amazed at how flavorful this dish is considering its small number of ingredients. I often roast the squash the night before to make this a quick 15-minute dinner the next day.

MAKE CANDIED WALNUTS:

Preheat oven to 350°F. Line a baking tray with parchment and set aside.

In a small, shallow bowl, combine the brown sugar and salt. Place the walnuts in a strainer and rinse under running water. Shake off excess water, transfer nuts to the bowl, and toss to coat with the sugar. Spread the nuts evenly on the prepared baking tray and bake for 8 minutes, stirring once halfway. Remove the parchment with the walnuts and set aside to cool. Increase oven temperature to 400°F.

ROAST SQUASH:

Cut the squash in half lengthwise. Use a spoon to remove and discard the seeds and strings. Place 1 teaspoon olive oil in each cavity and season with salt and pepper. Rub the mixture all over the flesh and place cut-side down on the baking tray. Roast for 40 minutes until tender.

Flip the squash over and let sit on the tray for 10 minutes to cool. Use a fork to scrape up the strands of squash. Leave the strands in the shells and set aside.

SAUTÉ SQUASH:

In a large skillet, warm 2 teaspoons olive oil over medium heat. Add the shallots, rosemary, and garlic. Cook, stirring occasionally, for 2 minutes. Add the chickpeas, season with salt and pepper, and cook until warmed through, about 1 to 2 minutes. Add the squash strands and toss until blended and hot. Check for seasoning. Divide between two plates, garnish with the candied walnuts, and serve.

CANDIED WALNUTS

2 tablespoons dark
   brown sugar
⅛ teaspoon salt
½ cup raw walnut halves

SQUASH

1 small spaghetti squash
   (2–2 ½ pounds)
4 teaspoons olive oil,
   divided
salt and pepper to taste
2 tablespoons chopped
   shallots
1 teaspoon finely
   chopped rosemary
2 garlic cloves, minced
½ cup chickpeas, rinsed

CHICKPEA LOAF

YIELD: 1 (9×5×3-INCH) LOAF

INGREDIENTS

2 teaspoons olive oil

4 ounces cremini mushrooms, chopped

½ cup chopped yellow onion

2 garlic cloves, minced

1 teaspoon dried thyme

1 teaspoon dried oregano

½ teaspoon salt

¼ teaspoon celery salt

⅛ teaspoon pepper

¼ cup vegetable broth

2 tablespoons vegan Worcestershire

1 tablespoon tomato paste

1 cup panko breadcrumbs

½ cup raw pecan halves

1 (15-ounce) can chickpeas

¼ cup organic ketchup

This chickpea loaf has all the classic meatloaf flavors—without any animal products. It has great texture from chickpeas and pecans and amazing umami from mushrooms, tomato paste, and vegan Worcestershire. Perfect for both weeknight suppers and holiday gatherings, this vegan meatloaf will impress even the most devout carnivores.

DIRECTIONS

Preheat oven to 350°F. Line a 9×5×3-inch pan with overhanging parchment and set aside.

In a medium pan, warm 2 teaspoons olive oil over medium heat. Add the mushrooms, onion, garlic, thyme, oregano, salt, celery salt, and pepper. Cook, stirring occasionally, for 5 to 6 minutes until mushrooms are tender and any liquid released by the mushrooms has evaporated. Remove from heat and stir in the broth, Worcestershire, and tomato paste. Set aside to cool.

In a large bowl, add the breadcrumbs. Place the pecans in a food processor, pulse until finely chopped, and add them to the breadcrumbs. Place a strainer over a small bowl (to catch the aquafaba) and drain the chickpeas. Rinse the chickpeas and add them to the food processor. Pulse until broken down into small pieces and add them to the breadcrumb-pecan mixture along with 6 tablespoons of aquafaba and the mushrooms. (You can freeze leftover aquafaba for 3 months.) Stir until combined and pat into the prepared pan.

Spread the ketchup on top and bake for 40 minutes. Let sit for 10 minutes before removing from pan and slicing. Delicious served as a sandwich or with mashed potatoes.

CITRUS DRESSING

2 tablespoons orange juice

2 teaspoons lemon juice

2 teaspoons maple syrup

1 teaspoon Dijon mustard

½ teaspoon orange zest

1 tablespoon extra-virgin olive oil

salt and pepper to taste

GRAIN

3 cups salted water

½ cup farro, rinsed

VEGETABLE

2 cups chopped butternut squash (½-inch cubes)*

1 tablespoon olive oil

¼ teaspoon garlic powder

¼ teaspoon salt

⅛ teaspoon pepper

PROTEIN

4 ounces extra-firm tofu, frozen and thawed

2 tablespoons cornstarch

2 tablespoons olive oil

⅛ teaspoon salt

GREENS

2 cups chopped baby spinach

2 tablespoons thinly sliced red onion

TOPPING

2 tablespoons toasted pumpkin seeds

2 tablespoons pomegranate arils

2 tablespoons chopped parsley

Can be substituted with Kabocha squash.

FARRO BOWL

GLUTEN-FREE | YIELD: 2 SERVINGS

This nutritious bowl showcases the best of autumn with roasted butternut squash, pumpkin seeds, pomegranate, tender farro, and crisp tofu on a bed of fresh spinach. A drizzle of citrus dressing completes the dish.

DIRECTIONS

Preheat oven to 400°F. Set aside a baking tray.

MAKE CITRUS DRESSING:

In a small bowl, whisk together orange juice, lemon juice, maple syrup, Dijon, and orange zest. Whisk in the olive oil until combined. Season with salt and pepper and set aside.

COOK GRAIN:

In a medium pot, bring 3 cups salted water to a boil over high heat. Add the farro, cover, and cook at a low boil for 25 minutes until grains are tender-chewy. Drain through a strainer, return farro to the pot, and cover to keep warm.

ROAST VEGETABLE AND COOK PROTEIN:

On the baking tray, toss the squash, olive oil, garlic powder, salt, and pepper. Spread out evenly and roast for 15 minutes. Stir and roast 5 minutes more.

While squash roasts, squeeze out as much water from the tofu as possible. Cut the tofu into 8 cubes. In a shallow bowl, stir the cornstarch, olive oil, and salt. Coat the tofu cubes with the slurry. Warm a medium skillet over medium-low heat. Cook the tofu cubes until crisp, about 2 minutes per side. Transfer to a plate and set aside.

BUILD BOWLS:

Fill two bowls with chopped spinach, red onion, farro, butternut squash, and tofu. Garnish with pumpkin seeds, pomegranate arils, and chopped parsley. Drizzle with the citrus dressing and serve.

RED BEANS & RICE

GLUTEN-FREE | YIELD: 2 SERVINGS

You won't miss the andouille sausage one bit! These red beans have amazing flavor and just the right amount of heat thanks to a perfect mix of spices and vegetables. At our home, this dish is incomplete without a bowl of freshly fried corn tortillas and some Red Rooster hot sauce.

THE DAY BEFORE, SOAK BEANS:
Place the beans in a medium bowl and cover with water by 2 inches. Soak for 24 hours.

THE NEXT DAY, COOK BEANS:
Drain and rinse the beans and set aside.
In a medium skillet, warm the olive oil over medium heat. Add the bell pepper, shallots, celery, and salt and cook, stirring occasionally, for 5 minutes until lightly caramelized. Add the garlic, chili, smoked paprika, oregano, thyme, cayenne, pepper, and bay leaf and cook for one minute. Stir in the broth, lemon juice, and beans. Bring to a boil, reduce heat, and cook, covered, at a low boil until beans are tender and most of the liquid has cooked off, about 1 hour and 15 minutes.

COOK RICE:
While the beans cook, combine the water, rice, oil, and seasoning in a small pot. Bring to a boil over medium heat, cover, and cook at a simmer for 15 minutes or until all the water is absorbed. Remove from heat and let sit for 10 minutes. Fluff and keep warm.

FINISH BEANS:
Turn off heat and remove bay leaf. Transfer ½ cup of the beans to a food processor and pulse a few times until mostly mashed. Add back to the skillet along with the scallion, chopped parsley, and vinegar, and stir until incorporated. Serve beans warm with the rice and hot sauce.

BEANS
½ cup dried red beans
water for soaking
2 teaspoons olive oil
½ cup small-diced green bell pepper
⅓ cup small-diced shallots
1 medium celery rib, small-diced
¼ teaspoon salt
2 garlic cloves, minced
1 tablespoon chopped chipotle chilis in adobo sauce
¼ teaspoon smoked paprika
⅛ teaspoon dried oregano
⅛ teaspoon dried thyme
pinch of cayenne pepper
pinch of black pepper
1 bay leaf
3 cups vegetable broth
1 teaspoon lemon juice
1 scallion, thinly sliced
2 tablespoons chopped parsley
1 teaspoon red wine vinegar

RICE
1 cup water
½ cup long-grain rice
½ teaspoon olive oil
½ teaspoon creole seasoning
hot sauce, for serving

POTATO PEA CURRY

GLUTEN-FREE | YIELD: 2 SERVINGS

INGREDIENTS

2 teaspoons olive oil

⅓ cup small-diced onion

1 garlic clove, minced

1 teaspoon grated ginger

1 teaspoon curry powder

½ teaspoon turmeric

½ teaspoon salt

pinch of cayenne
(optional for heat)

1 (10-ounce) Yukon
gold potato, cut into
¼-inch-thick pieces

1 teaspoon tomato paste

1 cup vegetable broth

½ cup coconut milk

½ cup frozen peas

2 tablespoons chopped
cilantro

This easy, one-pot potato pea curry makes a great weeknight dinner. It's pantry-friendly and goes from stove to table in fewer than 30 minutes. Serve over warm basmati rice to soak up the yummy coconut curry sauce.

DIRECTIONS

In a medium skillet, warm 2 teaspoons olive oil over medium heat. Add the onion, garlic, and ginger and cook, stirring, for 2 minutes. Add the curry powder, turmeric, salt, and cayenne and cook for 15 seconds. Stir in the potatoes and tomato paste and cook for 2 minutes. Add the broth, cover, and cook at a medium boil until potatoes are just tender, about 15 minutes. Stir in the coconut milk and peas. Continue cooking, uncovered, until warmed through and sauce reaches desired thickness. Fold in the chopped cilantro and serve.

STUFFED JERK POBLANOS

GLUTEN-FREE | YIELD: 2 SERVINGS

This immensely satisfying dish is always a big hit. Charred poblano peppers are stuffed with a super flavorful filling of pomegranate quinoa and jerk-marinated tempeh. A bright, creamy avocado cilantro sauce tops it all off.

PREPARE TEMPEH AND JERK MARINADE:

Cut the tempeh into ½-inch cubes and place in a steamer basket. Place over boiling water and steam for 15 minutes.

Meanwhile, prepare marinade by combining all the ingredients in a small bowl. Transfer half of the marinade into a small pot (for cooking the quinoa). When tempeh is done steaming, transfer the tempeh cubes to the bowl of remaining marinade, stir to coat, and set aside.

MAKE QUINOA:

Add the water and quinoa to the small pot, and stir to combine with the marinade. Bring to a simmer over medium heat and cook, covered, for 22 minutes or until all the water is absorbed. Keep covered and remove from heat.

PREPARE PEPPERS:

Turn oven on to broil. Rub the poblanos with ¼ teaspoon oil and place on a parchment-lined baking tray. Place tray under broiler and use tongs to turn the poblanos every 2 to 3 minutes until all sides are evenly charred. Place roasted poblanos in a bowl, cover with plastic wrap, and let sit for 3 minutes. Using your hands (I recommend wearing plastic gloves), peel off the skin. Make one lengthwise cut in each poblano, remove seeds, and place in a baking dish.

TEMPEH
4 ounces tempeh
water for steaming

JERK MARINADE
2 tablespoons olive oil
1 teaspoon coconut sugar
1 teaspoon dried thyme
1 teaspoon apple cider vinegar
½ teaspoon garlic powder
½ teaspoon chili powder
¼ teaspoon dried oregano
¼ teaspoon cinnamon
¼ teaspoon salt
¼ teaspoon pepper

QUINOA
1 cup water
⅓ cup quinoa
2 tablespoons pomegranate arils
2 tablespoons chopped cilantro
¼ cup salsa (store-bought or recipe on page 178)

PEPPERS
2 poblano peppers
¼ teaspoon olive oil

(Ingredients and Directions continued on page 120)

AVOCADO CILANTRO SAUCE

1 small ripe avocado, halved and pitted

⅓ cup chopped cilantro, packed

1 garlic clove, minced

2 tablespoons water

½ teaspoon apple cider vinegar

½ teaspoon lemon juice

¼ teaspoon salt

BAKE TEMPEH:
Turn oven to 400°F. Discard parchment and replace with new one. Spread the marinated tempeh on the sheet tray and bake for 25 minutes. Set aside.

STUFF POBLANOS:
Add 2 tablespoons pomegranate arils, 2 tablespoons chopped cilantro, and the baked tempeh to the quinoa and stir until combined. Season with salt and pepper. Use a large spoon to fill the poblanos, then top with salsa. Bake for 20 minutes until warmed through.

MAKE AVOCADO CILANTRO SAUCE:
Scoop out the avocado flesh and add to a food processor along with the remaining ingredients. Serve with the stuffed poblanos.

STUFFED ACORN SQUASH

YIELD: 2 SERVINGS

Creamy, roasted acorn squash is filled with a savory mushroom quinoa to create a hearty, healthy entrée. A buttery parmesan panko crust adds a wonderfully crisp texture while parsley, sage, and thyme add warmth to every bite.

DIRECTIONS
Preheat oven to 425°F and set aside a baking tray.

ROAST SQUASH:
Cut squash in half. Use a spoon to scrape out the seeds and strings. Place cut-side up on the baking tray and coat all over with 1 tablespoon olive oil. Season the flesh with salt and pepper. Roast for 30 minutes.

COOK QUINOA:
In a small pot, combine the water, quinoa, and oil. Bring to a simmer over medium heat and cook, covered, for 22 minutes or until all the water is absorbed. Keep covered and remove from heat.

PREPARE TOPPING:
In a small bowl, mix the panko, parmesan, and paprika. Stir in the melted butter and set aside.

SQUASH
1 acorn squash
1 tablespoon olive oil
salt and pepper

QUINOA
1 cup water
⅓ cup red quinoa
1 teaspoon olive oil

TOPPING
¼ cup panko
2 tablespoons grated
   vegan parmesan
¼ teaspoon paprika
2 teaspoons vegan
   unsalted butter,
   melted

(*Ingredients and Directions continued on 122*)

FILLING

2 teaspoons olive oil

1 cup sliced cremini
   mushrooms (¼ inch
   thick)

1 medium celery rib,
   small-diced

2 tablespoons minced
   shallots

1 garlic clove, minced

¼ teaspoon salt

⅛ teaspoon pepper

2 tablespoons chopped
   parsley

2 teaspoons chopped
   sage

1 teaspoon chopped
   thyme

3 tablespoons vegetable
   broth

MAKE FILLING:

In a medium skillet, warm 2 teaspoons olive oil over medium heat. Add the mushrooms, celery, shallots, garlic, salt, and pepper. Cook, stirring occasionally, for 3 minutes. Stir in the parsley, sage, and thyme and cook for 1 minute. Stir in the vegetable broth. Turn off heat and add the quinoa. Stir until combined and taste for seasoning.

STUFF SQUASH:

Use a large spoon to fill the squash with the quinoa mixture, pressing the quinoa into the cavity. Cover with panko topping. Return to oven for 5 minutes until tops are golden brown. Serve warm.

COLLARD GREENS & BEANS

GLUTEN-FREE | YIELD: 2 SERVINGS

INGREDIENTS

1 (8–10 ounces) bunch
   collard greens,
   chopped

½ cup water

½ cup olive oil

4 garlic cloves, minced

¾ teaspoon grated ginger

½ teaspoon smoked
   paprika

½ teaspoon salt

1 (15-ounce) can Great
   Northern beans,
   drained and rinsed

You don't need ham hocks to make intensely flavorful collard greens. Instead, cook them in a flavorful broth of garlic, ginger, and smoked paprika. To bulk up the dish, I add Great Northern beans for extra protein and fiber. Serve this dish over rice or with mashed potatoes for an easy, casual weeknight dinner.

DIRECTIONS

In a medium pot, combine all the ingredients *except for the beans*. Bring to a boil over high heat. Stir and reduce the heat to a low boil. Cover and cook for 40 minutes, stirring occasionally. Stir in the beans and cook, covered, until they are warmed through, about 5 minutes. Serve warm.

SLOW-COOKED SUMMER VEGETABLES

GLUTEN-FREE | YIELD: 2 SERVINGS

This easy one-pan meal is my take on briam, a traditional vegetable dish seen all across the Greek islands. Potato, eggplant, zucchini, tomato, fennel, bell pepper, and onion are slow-cooked in the oven until richly flavored and melt-in-your-mouth tender.

DIRECTIONS

Preheat oven to 400°F. Set aside a 9×13–inch baking dish.

Peel and cut the potato into ¼-inch-thick pieces and place them in the baking dish. Slice the eggplant into ½-inch-thick half-moons and add to the dish. Cut the zucchini into ½-inch-thick coins and add to the dish along with the tomato, fennel, bell pepper, red onion, and garlic.

Drizzle the top with extra-virgin olive oil, vegetable broth, sugar, salt, and pepper. Stir until all ingredients are evenly mixed. Cover with foil and bake for 40 minutes. Remove foil and bake 30 minutes more.

INGREDIENTS

1 small (8-ounce) Yukon gold potato

1 small (8-ounce) globe eggplant

1 small (6-ounce) zucchini

1 Roma tomato, cut into ½-inch-thick pieces

½ cup (½-inch) chopped fennel*

⅓ cup (½-inch) chopped green bell pepper

⅓ cup (½-inch) chopped red onion

2 garlic cloves, pressed

⅓ cup extra-virgin olive oil

¼ cup vegetable broth

1 teaspoon sugar

½ teaspoon salt

¼ teaspoon pepper

*I like to use a mix of fronds and stems and save the bulb for salads.

KALE PESTO

3 cups torn kale leaves, lightly packed

¼ cup chopped parsley, lightly packed

¼ cup roasted, salted almonds

2 tablespoons nutritional yeast

½ teaspoon lemon zest

1 garlic clove, peeled and smashed

¼ cup extra-virgin olive oil

salt and pepper to taste

CAULIFLOWER AND LENTILS

1 (2-pound) head of cauliflower

1½ tablespoons olive oil

¼ teaspoon garlic powder

¼ teaspoon turmeric

¼ teaspoon salt

2 garlic cloves, skin on

2 tablespoons almond milk

½ cup canned brown lentils*, drained and rinsed

If starting with raw lentils, cook scant ¼ cup in boiling water for 20 minutes to yield ½ cup cooked lentils.

ROASTED CAULIFLOWER STEAKS

GLUTEN-FREE | YIELD: 2 SERVINGS

This is one of my favorite meals to make—and eat. The recipe calls for a head of cauliflower—prepared two different ways. One half is sliced into steaks and roasted at high heat until caramelized, nutty, and buttery. The other half is boiled and pureed with roasted garlic and almond milk until smooth and creamy. Tender lentils and a bright, flavorful kale pesto complete the dish.

DIRECTIONS

Preheat oven to 400°F. Set aside a baking tray.

MAKE KALE PESTO:

Add the kale, parsley, almonds, yeast, lemon zest, and garlic to a food processor and blend until finely chopped. Add the olive oil 1 tablespoon at a time, pulsing after each addition. Season with salt and pepper.

COOK CAULIFLOWER AND LENTILS:

Remove the outer green leaves and slice off the bottom. Cut the cauliflower into ½-inch-thick "steaks." Choose about a half's worth of the cauliflower to use as steaks—typically the ones in the center hold their shape best—and transfer them to the baking tray. In a small bowl, combine the olive oil, garlic powder, turmeric, and salt. Rub the mixture all over the steaks. Lightly rub oil on the garlic cloves and place on the tray off to the side (this is for the cauliflower puree). Roast for 15 minutes, remove garlic cloves from oven, flip cauliflower steaks over, and cook 10 minutes more.

While the steaks and garlic cloves roast, cut the remaining cauliflower into small florets and transfer them to a medium pot. Cover with 1 inch of water and bring to a boil over high heat. Cook until tender, about 10 to 15 minutes. Drain in a strainer, dry out the pot, and return florets back to the pot. Peel and mash

(Continued)

128

the roasted garlic cloves and add to the pot along with the almond milk. Use an immersion blender to puree until smooth. Season with salt and pepper.

ASSEMBLE DISH:
Spoon the puree onto two plates and cover with the cauliflower steaks. Warm the lentils in the microwave. Spoon them off to the side of the puree and scatter the kale pesto generously on top.

SESAME SOBA NOODLES

GLUTEN-FREE | YIELD: 2 SERVINGS

These easy-to-make soba noodles are coated in a super flavorful ginger tamari sesame dressing, topped with perfectly roasted caramelized vegetables and juicy tomatoes. This is one of my favorite summertime meals.

DIRECTIONS
Preheat oven to 400°F. Lightly grease a baking sheet.

MAKE SAUCE:
In a large bowl, whisk the sauce ingredients together and set aside.

COOK NOODLES:
Fill a large bowl halfway with ice water and set a colander in the sink. In a medium pot, bring 5 cups of water to a boil over high heat. Add the noodles and cook at a medium boil for 4 minutes, stirring occasionally. Drain the noodles in the colander and transfer them to the ice bath. Vigorously swirl the noodles around with your fingers to rinse off excess starch. Drain the noodles in the colander and shake off excess water. Transfer the noodles to the sauce, stir to coat, and place in the refrigerator to chill while you roast the vegetables.

SAUCE
¼ cup olive oil
2 tablespoons coconut sugar
2 tablespoons white wine vinegar
2 tablespoons sesame oil
2 tablespoons tamari
1 tablespoon finely chopped shallots
1 teaspoon grated ginger
1 garlic clove, pressed

NOODLES
ice bath
5 cups water for boiling
6 ounces buckwheat soba noodles

(Ingredients and Directions continued on 133)

MAKE VEGETABLES AND GARNISHES:

In a large bowl, mix the broccoli florets, mushrooms, olive oil, salt, and pepper. Evenly spread them on the prepared tray and roast for 20 minutes, stirring once halfway.

While the vegetables roast, place 2 teaspoons sesame seeds in a small pan over medium heat. Shaking the pan frequently, toast the seeds for 3 to 5 minutes until golden brown. Transfer seeds to a small bowl and set aside.

SERVE:

Divide the noodles between two bowls. Arrange the roasted vegetables and fresh tomatoes on top. Garnish with chopped cilantro and toasted sesame seeds.

VEGETABLES

3 cups broccoli florets

4 cremini mushrooms, quartered

2 teaspoons olive oil

¼ teaspoon salt

⅛ teaspoon pepper

1 cup cherry (or grape) tomatoes, halved

GARNISHES

2 teaspoons sesame seeds

2 tablespoons chopped cilantro

DIPPING SAUCE

½ teaspoon sesame seeds

1 garlic clove, minced

2 tablespoons sesame oil

1 tablespoon + 1 teaspoon less-sodium soy sauce

1 tablespoon rice vinegar

2 teaspoons maple syrup

½ teaspoon grated ginger

¼ teaspoon chili garlic sauce

DUMPLINGS

2 teaspoons less-sodium soy sauce

½ teaspoon sesame oil

¼ teaspoon sugar

3 teaspoons olive oil, divided

2 scallions, thinly sliced, separate white from green parts

1 cup shredded carrot

1 cup finely chopped green cabbage

1 cup finely chopped mushrooms (cremini or shiitake)

salt and pepper to taste

1 garlic clove, minced

½ teaspoon finely grated ginger

16–20 gyoza dumpling wrappers

water for moistening and cooking

VEGETABLE DUMPLINGS

YIELD: 2 SERVINGS

These crazy good dumplings are filled with a rich mix of cabbage, carrots, mushrooms, and scallions. Served with a tasty sesame soy dipping sauce, these bite-sized delicacies are steamed and pan-fried to crispy perfection.

MAKE DIPPING SAUCE:

In a small pan, toast the sesame seeds over medium-low heat until golden brown. Transfer them to a small bowl and add the remaining ingredients. Whisk until incorporated and set aside.

MAKE DUMPLINGS:

In a small bowl, stir together the soy sauce, sesame oil, and sugar. Set aside.

In a medium pan, warm 1 teaspoon olive oil over medium heat. Add the white parts of the scallions, carrot, cabbage, and mushroom and season with salt and pepper. Cook for 6 to 7 minutes, stirring occasionally, until the vegetables are tender. Add the green parts of the scallion, garlic, and ginger, and cook for 2 minutes. Add the soy sauce mixture and stir until evaporated, about 30 seconds. Transfer mixture to a bowl.

Place about 1 tablespoon of filling onto the center of a dumpling wrapper. Lightly brush the edges with water. Fold in half and pinch the center. Place the dumpling on the counter to flatten the bottom. Wet the left side and fold 2 to 3 pleats from the center out. Repeat on the right side. Gently press folds to seal. Repeat this step with the remaining filling.

COOK DUMPLINGS:

In a large skillet, warm 2 teaspoons olive oil over medium heat. Arrange the dumplings evenly in the pan and cook for 2 to 3 minutes until bottoms are golden brown. Standing back, add 2 tablespoons water, cover with lid, and let steam for 2 to 3 minutes until most of the water has evaporated. Remove lid and cook off any excess water. Serve warm with the dipping sauce.

Alternate boiling method: Bring a medium pot of water to a boil over high heat. Add the dumplings and cook for 3 to 4 minutes.

ARTICHOKE CASSEROLE

YIELD: 2 SERVINGS

Ooh la la! That's what you'll be exclaiming with one bite of this warm, hearty casserole. Artichokes have a meaty mouthfeel that makes this dish incredibly satisfying.

DIRECTIONS
Preheat broiler to high. Set aside a small (1-quart) baking dish.

DRY ARTICHOKES:
Drain the artichokes in a mesh strainer. Gently squeeze them to remove excess water. Slice in quarters and lay cut-side down on two layers of paper towels to dry.

PREPARE TOPPING:
In a small bowl, mix the panko, parmesan, and parsley. Stir in the melted butter and set aside.

COOK PASTA:
In a medium pot, bring salted water to a boil. Cook the pasta according to package directions. Drain, rinse, and set aside.

MAKE CASSEROLE:
In a medium pot, melt 2 tablespoons butter over medium heat. Add the onions and cook until translucent, about 3 to 4 minutes. Add the flour and cook for 1 minute. Whisk in the almond milk, garlic powder, salt, and pepper. Bring to a low boil and cook for 1 minute until mixture slightly thickens. Add the parmesan, parsley, artichokes, and pasta and mix well. Taste for seasoning. Continue cooking for about 2 minutes until warmed through. Transfer to the baking dish and cover with the panko topping. Broil the top for 1 to 2 minutes until golden brown, rotating the dish for even browning. Serve warm.

INGREDIENTS
1 (14-ounce) can whole artichoke hearts

TOPPING
¼ cup panko
2 tablespoons grated vegan parmesan
1 teaspoon chopped parsley
1 tablespoon vegan salted butter, melted

PASTA
salted water for boiling
4 ounces elbow pasta

CASSEROLE
2 tablespoons vegan salted butter
½ cup small-diced onions
4 teaspoons all-purpose flour
1½ cups almond milk
½ teaspoon garlic powder
½ teaspoon salt
¼ teaspoon pepper
½ cup grated vegan parmesan
¼ cup chopped parsley

NOURISHING SOUPS

This chapter includes delicious vegetable and grain soups that boost the immune system, nourishing both body and soul. Comfort in a cup, soups are a great way to stay hydrated and full. From light broths to hearty cold-weather warmers, these soups get the job done without the meat and dairy. Satisfaction guaranteed!

RAMEN

GLUTEN-FREE | YIELD: 2 SERVINGS

This is a simple and appetizing healthy ramen with tofu. The slightly spicy broth is deeply flavored from caramelized onions, mushrooms, and miso. Finished with scallions and drops of chili sesame oil, this completely satisfying ramen will not disappoint.

DIRECTIONS

In a medium pot, warm the olive oil over medium heat. Add the onions and brown sugar. Reduce heat to medium-low and cook the onions, stirring occasionally, for 7 to 8 minutes until caramelized. Stir in the mushrooms and cook until lightly charred, about 3 minutes. Add the garlic, miso, tomato paste, and sriracha, and cook for 1 minute. Add the broth and tofu and stir until combined. Cover and simmer for 10 minutes. Set aside.

Cook the ramen noodles (without the spice packet) according to package directions. Drain and divide the noodles between two bowls. Top with the tofu-mushroom broth and garnish with scallions and drops of sesame chili oil.

INGREDIENTS

1 teaspoon olive oil

½ cup small-diced onion

2 teaspoons brown sugar

1 cup (½-inch-thick) sliced cremini mushrooms

3 garlic cloves, pressed

2 teaspoons miso

1 teaspoon tomato paste

1 teaspoon sriracha

3 cups vegetable broth, warm

7–8 ounces medium-firm tofu, cut into ¾-inch cubes

2 (2.8-ounce) packages rice ramen noodles*

1 scallion, thinly chopped

sesame chili oil for garnish

*I like Lotus Foods.

BONELESS BROTH

GLUTEN-FREE | OIL-FREE | YIELD: 2 SERVINGS (ABOUT 2½ CUPS)

INGREDIENTS

1 teaspoon black
  peppercorns
8 cups filtered water,
  divided
1 ounce dried shiitake
  mushrooms
½ ounce dried seaweed
4 garlic cloves, peeled
  and chopped
1 small onion, skin on and
  quartered
1 bay leaf
2 ounces garlic chives
  (with buds and stems)*
1 ounce parsley (with stems)
½ ounce turmeric, peeled
  and chopped
½ ounce ginger, peeled
  and chopped
1 tablespoon apple cider
  vinegar
1 teaspoon salt
cheesecloth for straining

*You'll find garlic chives sold in
bunches at Asian grocery stores.
Use them in soups, salads,
marinades, dips, or in stir-fries
as you would scallions or chives.

This is my plant-based version of bone broth. I sip on this soothing concoction during the cooler months for a boost of healing nutrients and antioxidants from mushrooms, seaweed, turmeric, garlic, and ginger. I often double the batch and use it as a substitute for vegetable broth when cooking.

DIRECTIONS

In a large pot over medium heat, toast the peppercorns until fragrant. Turn off heat and add 2 cups of filtered water, dried mushrooms, and seaweed. Submerge the vegetables and let soak for 15 minutes. Add the remaining ingredients to the pot along with 6 cups of filtered water. Bring to a boil then reduce to a simmer and cook uncovered for 90 minutes, stirring occasionally. Strain the broth through cheesecloth. Gather the edges on top and twist to squeeze out all the broth. Cool completely before storing in the refrigerator for up to two weeks or freeze for longer storage.

CHICKPEA & SWEET POTATO MULLIGATAWNY

GLUTEN-FREE | YIELD: 2 SERVINGS

Chunky and comforting with a warm blend of spices, this mulligatawny is soothing and nourishing. This is one of my all-time favorite soup recipes.

DIRECTIONS

In a medium pot, warm the olive oil over medium heat. Add the cinnamon stick and cumin seeds, and let sizzle for 10 seconds. Add the onions, celery, and carrot. Cook, stirring occasionally, for 10 minutes. Reduce heat as needed to prevent scorching.

Add the sweet potato, ginger, and garlic, and cook for one minute. Stir in the chickpeas, water, coconut milk, tomatoes, paprika, curry powder, salt, chili powder, sugar, pepper, and nutmeg. Increase heat and bring to a boil. Cover and cook at a low boil for 10 minutes, stirring occasionally.

Stir in the raisins and lentils. Cover and cook for 10 minutes. Remove pot from heat, discard cinnamon stick, and stir in the cilantro. Serve warm.

INGREDIENTS

1 tablespoon olive oil

1-inch cinnamon stick

¼ teaspoon cumin seeds

¾ cup chopped yellow onion

1 medium celery rib, small-diced

1 medium carrot, small-diced

1 cup medium-diced sweet potato, peeled

1 tablespoon grated ginger

3 garlic cloves, minced

1 cup chickpeas, rinsed

1 cup water

½ cup coconut milk

½ cup canned crushed tomatoes

½ teaspoon paprika

½ teaspoon curry powder

½ teaspoon salt

¼ teaspoon chili powder

¼ teaspoon sugar

⅛ teaspoon pepper

⅛ teaspoon nutmeg

2 tablespoons dark raisins

2 tablespoons red lentils

1 tablespoon chopped cilantro

HEARTY VEGETABLE SOUP

GLUTEN-FREE | YIELD: 2 SERVINGS

INGREDIENTS

1 small carrot, cut into ½-inch-thick coins

1 small zucchini, cut into ½-inch-thick coins

½ cup cauliflower florets

4 teaspoons olive oil, divided

½ teaspoon chopped rosemary

½ teaspoon chopped thyme plus one sprig

½ teaspoon salt, divided

⅛ teaspoon pepper

½ cup chopped onion

1 medium celery rib, small-diced

¼ cup shiitake or cremini mushrooms, quartered

¼ cup corn kernels (frozen is fine)

2 baby potatoes, cut into ½-inch-thick pieces

2 garlic cloves, minced

1 (9-ounce) Roma tomato

2 cups vegetable broth

½ cup chopped Swiss chard, packed

½ cup canned cannellini beans, drained and rinsed

Roasted vegetables are the stars of this nutritive soup. Roasting provides deep, sweet, caramelized flavor that boiling alone can't provide. Made with herbs and good-for-you veggies like potatoes, carrots, zucchini, Swiss chard, beans, and corn, this soup is hearty and satisfying.

ROAST VEGETABLES:

Preheat oven to 425°F. Set aside a baking tray.

In a large bowl, combine the carrot, zucchini, and cauliflower. Add 2 teaspoons olive oil, rosemary, ½ teaspoon chopped thyme, ¼ teaspoon salt, and pepper. Mix until vegetables are evenly coated. Spread the vegetables in a single layer on the baking tray. Roast for 20 minutes. Remove from oven and set aside.

MAKE SOUP:

In a medium pot, warm 2 teaspoons olive oil over medium heat. Add the onions, celery, and ¼ teaspoon salt. Cook, stirring occasionally, for 5 minutes until onions are translucent. Stir in the mushrooms, corn, potatoes, and garlic. Cook for 3 minutes. Grate the tomato across the largest holes of a box grater and add to the pot along with the broth and thyme sprig. Increase heat and bring to a boil. Cover, reduce to a simmer, and cook for 10 to 12 minutes until potatoes are tender. Stir in the chard, beans, and roasted vegetables. Cover and simmer for 2 minutes until warmed through. Discard thyme sprig, portion soup into two bowls, and serve.

CHANA DAL WITH GREENS

GLUTEN-FREE | YIELD: 2 SERVINGS

Dal is a staple Indian soup that can be made with different types of lentils. I like to use split brown chickpea lentils known as chana. They add a nutty flavor to the dal and maintain their shape after cooking, giving the dal great texture. Enjoy this soup as a light lunch or with Indian flatbread for a heartier meal.

DIRECTIONS

Place lentils in a strainer and rinse well with running water. Transfer to a medium pot with 2 cups water. Bring to a boil over high heat, reduce to a simmer, and skim off the white froth. Grate the tomato across the largest holes of a box grater and add to the pot along with the bay leaf, garlic, salt, turmeric, chili powder, and paprika. Cover with a lid, and cook at a low boil for 45 to 55 minutes until most of the water is absorbed and lentils are tender. Remove the bay leaf, add 1 cup water, and stir in the chopped greens. Cook, uncovered, for 4 to 5 minutes until greens are tender. Remove pot from heat.

In a small pan, warm the olive oil over medium-high heat. Add the chili, shallots, and cumin seeds. Cook for 2 to 3 minutes until the shallots turn golden brown. Stir into the dal and serve.

INGREDIENTS

½ cup chana dal lentils

3 cups water, divided

1 (7-ounce) Roma tomato

1 bay leaf

2 garlic cloves, minced

½ teaspoon salt

¼ teaspoon turmeric

¼ teaspoon chili powder

¼ teaspoon paprika

2 cups chopped greens, packed (e.g., chard, mustard, beet)

1 tablespoon olive oil

1 Thai green chili, chopped

¼ cup thinly sliced shallots

¼ teaspoon cumin seeds

SQUASH

1 small (2–2 ½-pounds)
spaghetti squash
1 teaspoon olive oil
salt and pepper

SOUP

2 teaspoons olive oil
⅓ cup small-diced yellow
onion
1 medium carrot, small-
diced
1 medium celery rib,
small-diced
2 garlic cloves, minced
½ teaspoon salt, divided
1 cup tomato sauce
1 cup vegetable broth
½ cup water
1 teaspoon sugar
½ teaspoon dried basil
¼ teaspoon dried
oregano
¼ teaspoon dried thyme
⅛ teaspoon pepper
½ cup kidney beans
1 tablespoon chopped
basil (or parsley)

GARNISH

1 tablespoon extra-virgin
olive oil
1 garlic clove, minced
2 tablespoon grated
vegan parmesan

SPAGHETTI SQUASH SOUP

GLUTEN-FREE | YIELD: 2 SERVINGS

This soul-warming soup is perfect during the fall and winter months when spaghetti squash is in peak season. A fragrant tomato broth flavored with basil, oregano, and thyme is served with creamy kidney beans and tender strands of squash.

ROAST SQUASH:

Preheat oven to 400°F and set aside a baking tray.

Cut the squash in half lengthwise. Wrap and store one half in the refrigerator for another day. Use a spoon to remove and discard the seeds and strings. Place 1 teaspoon olive oil in the cavity and season with salt and pepper. Rub the mixture all over the flesh and place squash cut-side down on the baking tray. Roast for 40 minutes until tender.

Flip squash over on tray and let sit for 10 minutes to cool. Use a fork to scrape out the strands of squash. Divide the squash between two soup bowls and cover to keep warm.

COOK SOUP:

In a medium pot, warm 2 teaspoons olive oil over medium-low heat. Add the onions, carrot, celery, garlic, and ¼ teaspoon salt. Cook, stirring occasionally, for 5 minutes. Add the tomato sauce, broth, water, sugar, basil, oregano, thyme, pepper, and remaining ¼ teaspoon salt. Bring to a simmer and cook, covered, for 10 minutes. Stir in the beans and basil and cook 1 minute more until warmed through. Remove from heat and ladle the soup into the bowls of squash.

COOK GARNISH:

In a small skillet, warm 1 tablespoon extra-virgin olive oil over medium heat. Stir the minced garlic in the oil for 20 seconds then spoon over the soups. Garnish with grated parmesan and serve immediately.

SCRUMPTIOUS SIDES

Who doesn't love a great side? These quick and easy small dishes taste amazing on their own but also pair with just about anything. From Mediterranean coleslaw to baked yuca fries, you're all set.

Yellow Rice
155

Wild Rice with Brussels Sprouts
156

Indian-Style Potatoes
159

Roasted Okra
160

Charred Kale with Red Onions, Cumin & Coriander
163

Mediterranean Coleslaw
164

Celery Slaw
167

Stewed Green Beans
168

Baked Yuca Fries
171

Pasta Salad
172

YELLOW RICE

GLUTEN-FREE | YIELD: 2 SIDE SERVINGS

This is a simple way to add more turmeric—a powerful antioxidant—to your diet. Get ready to see how easy it is to turn ordinary rice into something delicious, healthy, and pretty.

DIRECTIONS

In a small pot, add all the ingredients and stir to incorporate. Bring the mixture to a boil over medium-high heat. Reduce to a simmer, cover, and cook for 10 minutes or until all the water is absorbed. Remove pot from heat and let sit for 10 minutes. Carefully remove the lid so condensation doesn't drip onto the rice. Discard the cardamom pods, fluff rice, and serve warm.

INGREDIENTS

¾ cup water

½ cup jasmine rice

½ teaspoon olive oil

½ teaspoon ground turmeric

¼ teaspoon ground cumin

2 cardamom pods

pinch of salt

WILD RICE WITH BRUSSELS SPROUTS

GLUTEN-FREE | YIELD: 2 SIDE SERVINGS

INGREDIENTS

2 cups lightly salted water

½ cup wild rice

1 bay leaf

1 tablespoon olive oil

¼ cup raw walnut halves

¾ cup thinly sliced Brussels sprouts

¼ cup small-diced onions

1 medium celery rib, small-diced

¼ teaspoon salt

⅛ teaspoon pepper

⅛ teaspoon dried thyme

⅛ teaspoon dried sage

1 garlic clove, minced

1 tablespoon dried cranberries

½ teaspoon white wine vinegar

This gorgeous rice dish is worthy of a holiday gathering but easy enough for any time of the year. Tender and nutty wild rice is cooked with sautéed Brussels sprouts, onions, celery, sweet cranberries, and pan-fried walnuts. It's a side dish that always gets rave reviews.

DIRECTIONS

In a small pot, combine 2 cups lightly salted water, rice, and bay leaf and bring to a boil over high heat. Cover and cook at a low boil for 40 minutes until rice is tender. Drain through a strainer and discard bay leaf. Return rice to the pot, and cover to keep warm.

In a large skillet, warm the olive oil over medium heat. Add the walnuts and cook, stirring, for 1 to 2 minutes until light golden brown. Use a slotted spoon to transfer the nuts to a plate. Add the Brussels sprouts, onions, celery, salt, pepper, thyme, and sage to the pan. Cook, stirring occasionally, for 3 minutes until softened. Stir in the garlic and cook for 1 minute. Add the wild rice, cranberries, and vinegar. Cook until warmed through, about 1 to 2 minutes. Fold in the walnuts and serve.

INDIAN-STYLE POTATOES

GLUTEN-FREE | YIELD: 2 SIDE SERVINGS

These Indian-style potatoes are super creamy and boldly flavored with panch phoron, an East Asia five-spice blend of fenugreek, nigella, cumin, black mustard, and fennel. I grew up eating this richly spiced dish, and it remains one of my favorite ways to enjoy potatoes.

DIRECTIONS

In a small pot, add the potatoes and cover with salted water by 1 inch. Stir in the turmeric. Bring to a boil over high heat and cook until the potatoes are fork tender, about 13 to 14 minutes. Drain and set aside.

In a small skillet, warm the olive oil over medium heat. Add the panch phoron, curry powder, and salt. Swirl to incorporate, and let sizzle for 5 seconds. Add the potatoes and toss to coat with the seeds. Increase heat to high and cook for 3 minutes, tossing the potatoes every minute. Transfer to a bowl, garnish with cilantro, and serve.

INGREDIENTS

8 ounces baby red potatoes, halved (quartered if large)

salted water for boiling

½ teaspoon turmeric

1 tablespoon olive oil

1 teaspoon panch phoron

¼ teaspoon curry powder

¼ teaspoon salt

chopped cilantro for garnish

ROASTED OKRA

GLUTEN-FREE | YIELD: 2 SIDE SERVINGS

INGREDIENTS

12 ounces fresh okra
(frozen works, too)

1 tablespoon olive oil

¼ teaspoon cumin seeds

¼ teaspoon salt

1 tablespoon chopped
shallots

Roasting is my favorite way to cook okra. The high heat gives okra a crispy-chewy texture devoid of any trademark viscosity, and the caramelized bits of shallots provide an addictive crunch.

DIRECTIONS

Preheat oven to 425°F. Line a baking tray with parchment and set aside.

Cut okra into ½-inch-thick slices and place them in a large bowl. Add the olive oil, cumin seeds, and salt and toss well. Transfer to the prepared baking tray, and evenly spread out in a single layer.

Roast for 10 minutes. Stir the shallots into the okra, and roast 10 minutes more. (If using frozen okra, you'll need to roast slightly longer.) Serve warm.

CHARRED KALE WITH RED ONIONS, CUMIN & CORIANDER

GLUTEN-FREE | YIELD: 2 SIDE SERVINGS

I've cooked kale many different ways. This recipe for evenly charred, deeply flavored kale remains my favorite.

DIRECTIONS

In a large skillet, warm 2 teaspoons olive oil over medium heat. Add the red onions and cumin seeds. Cook and stir for 30 seconds. Add the chopped kale, coriander, and salt. Cook, stirring, for 1 minute until greens have wilted. Spread the kale in a single layer. Let the leaves char by cooking them *undisturbed* for 30 to 40 seconds. Stir the kale, and repeat this step until all the greens are evenly charred (about 2 to 3 more times). Season with fresh lemon juice and serve warm.

INGREDIENTS

2 teaspoons olive oil

¼ cup thinly sliced red onions

¼ teaspoon cumin seeds

3 cups chopped kale, packed

½ teaspoon ground coriander

¼ teaspoon salt

lemon wedge for seasoning

MEDITERRANEAN COLESLAW

GLUTEN-FREE | OIL-FREE | YIELD: 2 SIDE SERVINGS

INGREDIENTS

2 tablespoons apple cider
vinegar

1½ teaspoons maple syrup

¼ teaspoon celery seed

¼ teaspoon salt

pepper to taste

1 small carrot, thinly
shaved

2 cups thinly shaved red
cabbage

¼ cup thinly shaved red
onion

¼ cup chickpeas, rinsed

1 tablespoon chopped
parsley

Of all the recipes in this chapter, this is the one I make most often. This healthy slaw makes a great side to so many different types of dishes. Make sure to use a mandoline to thinly shave the vegetables. It gives the slaw an irresistible, pleasantly light texture.

DIRECTIONS

In a medium bowl, stir together the vinegar, maple syrup, celery seed, salt, and pepper. Add the remaining ingredients and toss until evenly mixed. Serve immediately.

CELERY SLAW

GLUTEN-FREE | OIL-FREE | YIELD: 2 SIDE SERVINGS

Leftover celery seems to live perpetually in my refrigerator drawer, so I came up with this tangy, crunchy slaw to curb the waste. Salt and vinegar chip lovers, this one's for you!

DIRECTIONS

In a medium bowl, add the garlic, vinegar, and mustard and whisk to combine. Season with salt and pepper to taste. Add the celery, scallion, and dill and stir until incorporated. Best served within a few hours.

INGREDIENTS

3 garlic cloves, minced

2 tablespoons red wine vinegar

1 teaspoon Dijon mustard

salt and pepper to taste

2 cups chopped celery, diagonally sliced

2 tablespoons thinly sliced scallions

1 tablespoon chopped dill

STEWED GREENS BEANS

GLUTEN-FREE | YIELD: 2 SIDE SERVINGS

INGREDIENTS

1 tablespoon olive oil

½ cup thinly sliced onion

10 ounces green beans, trimmed

2 garlic cloves, peeled and sliced

½ teaspoon salt

¼ teaspoon paprika

⅛ teaspoon pepper

1 (7-ounce) Roma tomato

¼ cup vegetable broth

1 tablespoon chopped dill

This is an easy, slow-cooked dish made with green beans, tomatoes, garlic, and dill. As the green beans slowly cook, they soak up all the delicious flavors in the broth and become incredibly tender and juicy.

DIRECTIONS

In a large skillet, warm the olive oil over medium heat. Add the onions and cook, stirring, for 5 minutes until caramelized. Add the greens beans, garlic, salt, paprika, and pepper and cook for 2 minutes. Grate the tomato across the largest holes of a box grater and add to the pan along with the vegetable broth and dill. Cover and cook at a simmer for 30 to 35 minutes until beans are very tender. Transfer to a platter and serve warm.

BAKED YUCA FRIES

GLUTEN-FREE | YIELD: 2 SIDE SERVINGS

Give potatoes a break, and whip up a batch of yuca fries! They're soft and creamy on the inside and irresistibly crispy on the outside achieved by baking, not frying. Packed with carbs and fiber, yuca is a starchy root vegetable popular in Latin cooking. If you've never tried this tuber before, this side dish is a great introduction.

DIRECTIONS

Preheat oven to 425°F. Line a baking tray with parchment and set aside.

Cut off the ends of the yuca and cut into 2½- to 3-inch segments. Make a shallow lengthwise cut through the skin and peel off. Bring a medium pot of salted water to a boil over high heat. Add the yuca and cook until fork-tender but not falling apart, about 30 to 35 minutes. (The segments may split in half while boiling, which is okay.) Drain and set aside to cool for 5 minutes.

In a medium bowl, combine the olive oil, garlic powder, paprika, salt, and pepper and set aside.

Cut the yuca into ½-inch-thick wedges, removing the stringy fibrous core. Reserve half the wedges for a later date. (They keep well for up to a week in the refrigerator or 2 months in the freezer.) Place the remaining wedges in the bowl with the oil-spice mixture and stir to coat. Arrange the fries on the prepared tray. Bake for 10 minutes, flip fries over, and bake 5 minutes more. Serve immediately.

INGREDIENTS

1 (2½–3-pound) yuca

salted water for boiling

1 tablespoon olive oil

¼ teaspoon garlic powder

⅛ teaspoon paprika

⅛ teaspoon salt

pinch of pepper

PASTA SALAD

GLUTEN-FREE | YIELD: 2 SIDE SERVINGS

INGREDIENTS

1 tablespoon extra-virgin
  olive oil

1 tablespoon tahini

1 tablespoon water

1 teaspoon apple cider
  vinegar

1 teaspoon maple syrup

½ teaspoon country-style
  Dijon mustard

½ teaspoon lemon juice

salt and pepper to taste

salted water for boiling

3 ounces dried udon
  noodles*

2 tablespoons finely
  chopped green Italian
  long hot chili

1 tablespoon finely
  chopped red onion

I like Assi organic.

This is an easy and quick dish to make when you need a side, stat!
It's simple but super flavorful, and the dressing takes just a minute
or two to prepare. After a short boil, the noodles are tossed with
the dressing and ready to be served.

DIRECTIONS

In a medium serving bowl, add the olive oil, tahini, water, vinegar,
maple syrup, mustard, lemon juice, salt, and pepper. Stir until
combined and set aside.

Prepare an ice bath and set aside. Bring a medium pot of salted
water to a boil over high heat. Add the noodles and cook at a low
boil for 5 minutes until tender. Drain the noodles in a colander
and transfer to the ice bath. Vigorously swirl the noodles around
with your fingers to rinse off excess starch. Drain the noodles in
the colander and shake off excess water. Transfer noodles to the
bowl of dressing along with the green chili and red onion. Stir
until all ingredients are incorporated and serve.

NUTRITIOUS SNACKS AND DIPS

Get ready to dip, scoop, pick, and grab your way to some satisfying bites. From creamy dips to savory snacks, here are some yummy treats to satisfy all your midday or late-night cravings.

Pea Tapenade
177

Everyday Salsa
178

Baba Ghanoush
181

Marinated Olives
182

Pickled Vegetable Relish
185

Miso Guacamole
186

Energy Bars
189

Rye Pretzels
190

PEA TAPENADE

GLUTEN-FREE | YIELD: 2 SERVINGS (ABOUT 1 CUP)

This bright tapenade is made with heart-healthy peas, basil, garlic, and lemon and comes together in less than 10 minutes. Serve this creamy dip with bread, crudités, or crackers.

INGREDIENTS

1⅓ cups frozen peas

1 cup basil leaves, lightly packed

3 tablespoons extra-virgin olive oil

2 tablespoons grated vegan parmesan, plus more for garnish

1 teaspoon lemon juice

1 garlic clove, peeled

¼ teaspoon salt

⅛ teaspoon pepper

DIRECTIONS

Place the peas in a strainer and run under warm tap water for 30 seconds to defrost. Place half of the peas in a small food processor along with the basil, olive oil, 2 tablespoons parmesan, lemon juice, garlic, salt, and pepper. Process until smooth and scrape down the bowl as needed. Add the remaining peas and pulse until rough chopped. Transfer tapenade to a small bowl, garnish with parmesan, and serve.

EVERYDAY SALSA

GLUTEN-FREE | OIL-FREE | YIELD: 2 SERVINGS (ABOUT 2 CUPS)

INGREDIENTS
1 (14-ounce) can diced
   fire-roasted tomatoes
½ cup chopped cilantro
¼ cup chopped red onion
1 jalapeño, deseeded and
   chopped
3 garlic cloves, chopped
1 teaspoon coconut sugar
1 teaspoon lime juice
½ teaspoon smoked
   paprika
½ teaspoon salt
¼ teaspoon ground
   cumin
⅛ teaspoon pepper

This is my go-to salsa recipe. It's full of great flavor and is quickly made in the food processor. Mildly spicy, this salsa pairs perfectly with chips and is great served with the Stuffed Jerk Poblanos (page 119) and Jackfruit Burritos (page 80).

DIRECTIONS
Place all ingredients in a food processor and blend to desired consistency. Store in refrigerator or freeze.

BABA GHANOUSH

GLUTEN-FREE | YIELD: 2 SERVINGS

I became hugely obsessed with my local Greek restaurant's version of baba ghanoush, so I attempted to recreate it at home. Smoky and creamy, this is the ultimate baba ghanoush recipe.

ROAST GARLIC AND EGGPLANT:

Preheat the oven to 400°F. Line a baking tray with parchment and set aside.

Place the garlic cloves on a small piece of foil and drizzle lightly with olive oil. Wrap up the cloves and place on the prepared baking tray. Use a paring knife to make a few scattered 2-inch-deep slits in the eggplant. Place the eggplant directly over a medium gas flame on the stove to lightly char the skin, rotating with tongs as needed. (Alternatively, you can use an oven broiler to char the skin.) Transfer the eggplant to the baking tray and place in oven.

Roast the garlic for 20 minutes and remove from oven; roast the eggplant for 30 minutes, transfer the eggplant to a cutting board, and slice in half. Place the halves flesh-side down in a colander in the sink for 5 minutes to allow excess water to drain.

MAKE BABA GHANOUSH:

In a medium bowl, stir together the tahini, vinegar, salt, paprika, and cumin. Remove garlic from the foil, peel off skin, and mash the cloves on a cutting board with the side of a large knife. Add to the bowl and stir until combined.

Transfer the eggplant to the cutting board and remove the skin. Chop the flesh into small chunks and mix well with the tahini mixture. Transfer baba ghanoush to a small serving bowl and chill completely in the refrigerator. Drizzle with extra-virgin olive oil and garnish as desired before serving.

INGREDIENTS

2 garlic cloves (skin on)
olive oil
1 small globe eggplant
   (about 1 pound)
1 tablespoon tahini
1 teaspoon red wine
   vinegar
¼ teaspoon salt
⅛ teaspoon paprika
⅛ teaspoon ground
   cumin
extra-virgin olive oil,
   parsley, pine nuts,
   pomegranate arils,
   sesame seeds for
   garnish

MARINATED OLIVES

GLUTEN-FREE | YIELD: 1 (16-OUNCE) JAR

INGREDIENTS

¾ cup extra-virgin olive oil

2 garlic cloves, thinly sliced

1 (2-inch) strip lemon peel

1 rosemary sprig

1 bay leaf

⅛ teaspoon fennel seeds

⅛ teaspoon red chili flakes

⅛ teaspoon salt

10 ounces mixed olives (black and green)

Olives are a great snack full of healthy fats and antioxidants. These marinated olives keep for months in the refrigerator and make a great gift during the holidays.

DIRECTIONS

In a small pot, combine the olive oil, garlic, lemon peel, rosemary, bay leaf, fennel seeds, chili flakes, and salt. Warm over medium heat just until the garlic sizzles. Remove from heat.

Combine the olives in a large bowl. Rinse and drain well. Pack them in a 16-ounce mason jar. Slowly pour the olive oil mixture on top. If needed, top off with additional olive oil. Cover and let sit in the refrigerator for at least 48 hours to marinate.

Note: The olive oil will solidify as it chills, so bring to room temperature before serving.

PICKLED VEGETABLE RELISH

GLUTEN-FREE | YIELD: 1 (16-OUNCE) JAR

This is a great way to pickle all sorts of vegetables. You can leave them whole for snacking or chop them into a relish and use in sandwiches or salads.

DIRECTIONS

In a large bowl, toss the vegetables with ½ teaspoon salt. Transfer mixture to a colander and place the colander in the bowl. Set aside for 1 hour to brine.

Meanwhile, place the chili in a mug and cover with boiling water. Use a spoon to weigh down if needed. Let the chili rehydrate for 30 minutes. Drain and set aside.

In a 2-cup liquid measure, whisk the garlic, olive oil, vinegar, sugar, oregano, thyme, chili flakes, and celery salt. Pack the chili and brined vegetables (do not rinse) into a 16-ounce jar. Pour the pickling liquid on top, cover, and let sit in the refrigerator overnight.

The next day, use tongs to remove the vegetables and chop them into small pieces. Return them to the jar and store in the refrigerator for up to 2 weeks.

Note: The olive oil will solidify as it chills, so bring to room temperature before serving.

INGREDIENTS

8 ounces mixed cut vegetables*

½ teaspoon salt

1 dried guajillo chili

boiling water

2 garlic cloves, thinly sliced

½ cup extra-virgin olive oil

½ cup white vinegar

1 tablespoon coconut sugar

½ teaspoon dried oregano

¼ teaspoon dried thyme

⅛ teaspoon red chili flakes

⅛ teaspoon celery salt

Pictured are broccoli, cauliflower, cremini mushroom, celery, and carrot.

MISO GUACAMOLE

GLUTEN-FREE | OIL-FREE | YIELD: 2 SERVINGS

INGREDIENTS

1½ teaspoons white miso

½ teaspoon lime juice

1 garlic clove, minced

1 large avocado, halved
   and pitted

1 tablespoon finely
   chopped red onion

1 tablespoon chopped
   cilantro

pepper to taste

Miso guacamole is a fresh new take on a Mexican classic. The addition of miso adds salty, savory complexity—not to mention a slew of nutrients and gut-friendly bacteria.

DIRECTIONS

In a medium bowl, stir together the miso, lime juice, and garlic. Add the avocado flesh and mash to desired consistency. Fold in the red onion and cilantro. Season with pepper to taste.

ENERGY BARS

GLUTEN-FREE | OIL-FREE | YIELD: 2 BARS

These no-bake energy bars are one of my favorite healthy snacks to have on hand. They're perfect when you're craving something sweet or just need a boost of energy. The best part? They take fewer than 10 minutes to make.

DIRECTIONS

In a food processor, pulse dates 3 to 4 times until coarsely chopped. Add the remaining ingredients, *except for the cashew butter and chocolate*. Blend until lightly chopped. Transfer mixture to a large bowl. Add the cashew butter and chocolate chips. Use your hands to mix all the ingredients together and gather into a ball. On a cutting board, press and form the mixture into a 1-inch-thick rectangle (about 2×4 inches) and cut into two squares. Store covered in the refrigerator.

INGREDIENTS

½ cup chopped Medjool dates (about 5 large)

2 tablespoons whole pecans

1 tablespoon toasted pumpkin seeds

1 tablespoon oats

1 tablespoon raisins (golden or dark)

1 teaspoon sesame seeds

1 teaspoon chia seeds

¼ teaspoon cinnamon

¼ teaspoon vanilla extract

⅛ teaspoon salt

1 tablespoon cashew butter

1 tablespoon dark chocolate chips

RYE PRETZELS

YIELD: 2 PRETZELS

INGREDIENTS
⅓ cup warm water (110°F)
1 teaspoon brown sugar
¾ teaspoon active dry yeast
½ cup all-purpose flour
½ cup rye flour
1 tablespoon vegan butter, melted
½ teaspoon salt
5 cups water
¼ cup baking soda
coarse salt for sprinkling

Looking for a highly satisfying savory snack? These soft and chewy rye pretzels are it! I highly recommend having some mustard nearby for dipping.

DIRECTIONS

In an electric mixer bowl, stir together the warm water, brown sugar, and yeast. Let sit for 5 minutes for yeast to activate. Add the flours, melted butter, and salt and mix with the paddle attachment on low to medium speed for 3 minutes. Transfer dough to a lightly greased bowl. Cover and let rise until doubled in size, about 1 hour.

Preheat oven to 400°F. Line a baking tray with parchment and set aside.

Divide dough in half. Working with one piece at a time, use your palms to roll the dough on the counter into a 20-inch-long rope. Shape into a "U," intertwine the ends, bring the twisted ends toward you, and gently press the ends onto the bottom curve of the pretzel.

In a large sauté pan, bring 5 cups water to a boil over high heat. Add the baking soda (mixture will bubble). Immediately lay the pretzels in the water and let them boil for 45 seconds. Use a slotted spatula to transfer the pretzels onto a dish towel and dab them dry.

Transfer the pretzels to the prepared tray and sprinkle tops with some coarse salt. Bake for 10 to 11 minutes until pretzels are golden brown.

INDULGENT SWEETS

I've saved the best for last, my friends! From decadent classics like chocolate layer cake and brown sugar peanut butter cookies to seasonal favorites like strawberry marzipan galette and blueberry lavender crisp, this chapter is full of indulgent plant-based sweets that everyone will love. Enjoy!

CHOCOLATE CLUSTERS

GLUTEN-FREE | OIL-FREE | YIELD: 2 SERVINGS

It's hard to find a box of chocolates for two. My solution? Make them at home, of course! Packed with good-for-you seeds and almonds, these heart-healthy dark chocolate clusters are perfectly portioned for you and yours.

DIRECTIONS

Line a small tray or plate with parchment and set aside.

Warm a small, nonstick skillet over medium heat. Add the sesame, flax, and sunflower seeds. Stir frequently until toasted, about 3 to 4 minutes. Transfer to a small bowl and set aside.

Place the chocolate in a microwave-safe bowl. Melt the chocolate on low, stirring every 20 seconds. Add the seeds, chopped almonds, and cinnamon and stir until combined.

Drop two spoonfuls of the chocolate mixture onto the prepared tray. Shape them into ½-inch-tall rounds or ovals (they're easier to bite into at this height). Place in the refrigerator for 5 minutes, then transfer to a cool room to set up completely, about 1 hour. Store clusters in a covered container at room temperature.

INGREDIENTS

1½ teaspoons sesame seeds

1½ teaspoons flax seeds

1½ teaspoons raw sunflower seeds

1½ ounces dark chocolate, chopped

3 tablespoons roasted salted almonds, chopped

pinch of cinnamon

MEXICAN CHOCOLATE PUDDING PARFAITS

YIELD: 2 SERVINGS

GRAHAM CRUMBLE
2 tablespoons graham crumbs

1 teaspoon unsalted vegan butter, melted

½ teaspoon sugar

CHOCOLATE PUDDING
6 ounces silken tofu

3 ounces dark chocolate (60% or more), melted and cooled

3 tablespoons maple syrup

½ teaspoon cinnamon

½ teaspoon vanilla extract

¼ teaspoon chili powder

pinch of salt

COCONUT WHIPPED CREAM
1 (14-ounce) can coconut milk*, chilled overnight

1 tablespoon powdered sugar

*I recommend Aroy-D coconut milk.

This creamy pudding parfait is divine. Rich chocolate pudding and coconut whipped cream are layered with a delicate graham crumble, making every bite delightful.

DIRECTIONS
Preheat oven to 350°F. Line a baking tray with parchment and set aside. Place a mixing bowl in the refrigerator to chill.

MAKE GRAHAM CRUMBLE:
In a small bowl, add all the ingredients and mix with your hands until combined. Transfer to the prepared tray and use your hands to pat and shape into a rough 3-inch round. Bake for 7 minutes until golden brown. Set aside to cool.

MAKE CHOCOLATE PUDDING:
Place the tofu in a bowl and warm in the microwave for 30 seconds. Transfer to a blender along with the remaining ingredients and process until smooth. Divide the chocolate pudding between two (8-ounce) ramekins. Place in the refrigerator while you make the whipped cream.

MAKE COCONUT WHIPPED CREAM:
Open the can of coconut milk, scoop out the solidified coconut fat, and transfer it to the chilled mixing bowl. Using a stand or handheld mixer, beat on high for 30 seconds. Add the powdered sugar and beat 1 minute until thick and fluffy. Set aside.

Gently break the graham cookie into tiny pieces and crumbs. Reserve ½ teaspoon for garnish and sprinkle the remaining on top of the pudding. Spoon or pipe the whipped cream on top of the pudding and garnish with the reserved crumble. Let parfaits set up in the refrigerator for at least 1 hour before serving.

CHOCOLATE LAYER CAKE

YIELD: 1 TALL SLICE FOR 2

This is my favorite chocolate cake—vegan or otherwise. It's moist, tender, and ridiculously chocolatey. Perfectly portioned for two, this dreamy cake is great for anniversaries and intimate birthdays.

MAKE CAKE:

Preheat oven to 350°F. Lightly grease a 6-inch round pan and line the bottom with parchment.

In a medium bowl, combine the flour, sugar, cocoa powder, baking powder, baking soda, and salt and make a well in the center. In a small bowl, whisk together the almond milk, oil, maple syrup, vinegar, vanilla, and espresso powder. Pour the mixture into the well and whisk until smooth. Transfer batter to the prepared pan.

Bake for 16 minutes or until the center bounces back when gently pressed. Let cake rest 10 minutes. Invert cake and transfer to a wire rack to cool completely.

MAKE FROSTING:

In an electric mixer bowl fitted with the paddle attachment, beat the butter until smooth. Scrape down the bowl. Add the powdered sugar, cocoa powder, vanilla, and salt to the bowl. With the mixer on low speed, drizzle in the warm water. Increase speed to medium and beat until light and fluffy, scraping down the bowl as needed.

FROST CAKE:

When cake is completely cool, use a serrated knife to level off the top. Cut the cake into quarters (four equal wedges) and place one of the wedges on a dessert plate. Spread a thin layer of frosting on top and cover with another cake wedge. Continue to frost and stack, spreading a thicker layer of frosting on the last cake wedge. Can be served immediately or chilled.

CAKE

- ½ cup all-purpose flour
- ¼ cup sugar
- 3 tablespoons cocoa powder, sifted
- ½ teaspoon baking powder
- ¼ teaspoon baking soda
- ¼ teaspoon salt
- ½ cup almond milk
- 2 tablespoons olive oil
- 1 tablespoon maple syrup
- ½ teaspoon apple cider vinegar
- ½ teaspoon vanilla extract
- ¼ teaspoon espresso powder

FROSTING

- 2 tablespoons unsalted vegan butter, soft
- ½ cup powdered sugar
- ¼ cup cocoa powder, sifted
- ½ teaspoon vanilla extract
- pinch of salt
- 1½ tablespoons warm water

BLUEBERRY LAVENDER CRISPS

YIELD: 2 SERVINGS

STREUSEL
¼ cup all-purpose flour

1½ tablespoons sugar

1 tablespoon light brown sugar

pinch of salt

2 tablespoons unsalted vegan butter, cold and cubed

FILLING
¼ cup sugar

1½ tablespoons cornstarch

½ teaspoon dried lavender

2 cups blueberries

Blueberry and lavender make a beautiful pair. The floral notes of lavender bring out the sweetness in blueberry and add an elegant twist to this delicious crisp.

DIRECTIONS
Preheat oven to 350°F.

MAKE STREUSEL:
In a large bowl, stir together the flour, sugars, and salt. Add the cold, cubed butter and use a pastry cutter to break it down into small, pea-sized pieces. Place bowl in refrigerator while you make the filling.

MAKE FILLING:
In a medium bowl, whisk together the sugar, cornstarch, and lavender. Add *half* the blueberries and mash them with the back of a fork. Stir in the remaining blueberries.

BAKE CRISP:
Divide the blueberry filling between two (8-ounce) ramekins. Top with the streusel (do not pat down). Bake for 20 minutes. Turn broiler on high and cook for 1 to 2 minutes until tops are golden brown. Serve warm.

CARAMEL BREAD PUDDINGS

OIL-FREE | YIELD: 2 SERVINGS

Moist, dense, sweet, rich—this amazing bread pudding is so satisfying and decadent. It's warmly spiced with cinnamon and nutmeg and dotted with juicy raisins. The caramel sauce, made with coconut milk, is quick and easy to make.

DIRECTIONS
Preheat oven to 350°F. Set aside a baking tray.

MAKE CARAMEL SAUCE:
In a small pot, add 2 tablespoons sugar and place over medium-high heat. Allow sugar to melt undisturbed. Once sugar begins to turn golden brown in areas, gently and occasionally stir the sugar to promote even caramelization. When sugar has completely melted and turned a deep amber color, add the coconut milk in three parts, stirring after each addition. Continue to boil until slightly thickened. Remove from heat and season with salt to taste. Pour caramel into a small bowl and set aside.

MAKE BREAD PUDDING:
In a small bowl, whisk together the cornstarch, cinnamon, and nutmeg. Warm the coconut milk in the microwave for 30 seconds and add it to the bowl along with the maple syrup and vanilla. Whisk until all ingredients are incorporated.

Evenly distribute the bread cubes and raisins between two (8-ounce) ramekins. Pour the milk mixture evenly between ramekins and gently push down with the back of a fork to wet all the bread. Sprinkle tops with a little brown sugar.

Bake ramekins on the baking tray for 12 minutes until custard is set. Switch to broil and cook for 1 to 2 minutes until tops are lightly browned. Garnish with powdered sugar and serve warm with the caramel sauce.

CARAMEL SAUCE
2 tablespoons sugar
3 tablespoons coconut milk
salt to taste

BREAD PUDDING
1 teaspoon cornstarch
¼ teaspoon cinnamon
pinch of nutmeg
½ cup coconut milk
2 tablespoons maple syrup
½ teaspoon vanilla extract
2 cups (½-inch-cubed) whole wheat bread
1 tablespoon raisins
light brown sugar for sprinkling
powdered sugar for garnish

BROWN SUGAR
PEANUT BUTTER COOKIES

OIL-FREE | YIELD: 2 COOKIES

INGREDIENTS

¾ tablespoon warm water

¾ teaspoon flaxseed meal

3 tablespoons natural
  chunky peanut butter

3 tablespoons light
  brown sugar

1 tablespoon all-purpose
  flour

¼ teaspoon vanilla
  extract

⅛ teaspoon baking soda

⅛ teaspoon cinnamon

granulated sugar for
  rolling

These easy, one-bowl peanut butter cookies are soft, tender, and rich with brown sugar. They're made with natural chunky peanut butter for amazing flavor and perfectly portioned for your crowd of two.

DIRECTIONS

Preheat oven to 350°F. Line a baking tray with parchment and set aside.

In a medium bowl, mix the water and flaxseed meal. Let sit for 5 minutes to thicken.

Add the remaining ingredients to the bowl and mix until combined. Divide the dough in half, shape into balls, and coat with granulated sugar. Place on the prepared tray, flatten to about ½ inch thick, and use the back of a fork to create a crisscross pattern. Bake for 10 to 11 minutes until crackly on top and edges are set.

STRAWBERRY MARZIPAN GALETTE

YIELD: 1 (6-INCH) GALETTE

This gorgeous strawberry galette is a yummy combination of juicy fruit and flaky crust. A hidden layer of marzipan beneath the fruit adds sweet almond flavor to every bite.

DIRECTIONS
Preheat oven to 400°F. Line a baking tray with parchment.

MAKE DOUGH:
In a large bowl, combine flour, sugar, and salt. Add the butter and use a pastry cutter to break it down into pea-sized pieces. Sprinkle 3 tablespoons cold water on top. Using your hands, gather the mixture until it comes together to form a dough. Shape into a disc, wrap with plastic, and place in the refrigerator while you make the filling.

PREPARE FILLING:
Set aside 1 teaspoon of almonds. Add the remaining almonds to a small nonstick pan over medium heat. Toast the almonds until golden brown, about 5 minutes. Transfer almonds to a small bowl and set aside.

On a piece of parchment, roll out the marzipan to a 5½-inch round and set aside.

Hull and cut the strawberries in half (or quarters if large) and place in a large bowl. Add the sugar, flour, lemon zest, and lemon juice, and stir until incorporated.

ASSEMBLE GALETTE:
On a lightly floured surface, roll out the dough to a 9½-inch round and transfer it to the prepared baking tray. Spread the toasted almonds in the center of the dough, leaving a 2-inch

(Continued)

DOUGH
¾ cup all-purpose flour
1 teaspoon sugar
pinch of salt
5 tablespoons unsalted vegan butter, cold and cubed
3 tablespoons cold water

FILLING
2 tablespoons sliced almonds
1 ounce marzipan
8 ounces strawberries
1 tablespoon sugar
1 tablespoon all-purpose flour
½ teaspoon lemon zest
½ teaspoon lemon juice
½ teaspoon almond milk
½ teaspoon maple syrup
2 teaspoons strawberry preserves

border all around. Lay the marzipan on top of the almonds. Cover with the strawberries. Fold the edges of dough inward, leaving the center exposed.

In a small bowl, stir the almond milk and maple syrup until combined. Brush on the crust and sprinkle with the reserved almonds.

Bake for 30 to 35 minutes until crust is lightly browned and filling bubbles. Warm the strawberry preserves in the microwave for a few seconds and gently brush on the berries. Let galette cool for at least 10 minutes before slicing.

ACKNOWLEDGMENTS

I have to be honest, I love writing cookbooks, but I don't sit around all day thinking about what my next cookbook will be. Fortunately, I have a fantastic agent, Deborah Ritchken, who always seems to check in at the right time, nudging me to start thinking. She took a chance on me eight years ago when I was a small business owner who wanted to share my bakery's recipes in a book. Since then, she has supported and encouraged me to continue writing cookbooks—and this one is my fifth. Her enthusiasm and ever-flowing ideas always get me excited about my next book.

There were times when I didn't think this book would happen. I knew I wanted to write a book that reflected the food I was eating at home, but I struggled with the framework. Finally, after months of thoughtful consideration and bouncing around multiple ideas, this book began coming together. My editor Nicole Frail worked with me to nail down the concept and believed that I could write it. I developed the recipes with enthusiasm and obsession, which led to post-deadline tweaks, additions, and deletions. Nicole was always open to my changes, and for that, I am so appreciative.

I know that multiple people at Skyhorse Publishing worked on this book. They always do such a great job, and I'm so thankful for their contributions.

Everyone loves cookbooks with lots of photos. I did my best to photograph the food, but I needed someone more skilled to handle the visual branding. I was fortunate enough to meet Kaysha Weiner, and it turned out that working with her was the most fun part of writing this book! She perfectly captured the look and feel of both my professional and personal life. I cannot wait to work with her again.

Life—and cookbook photoshoots—are better when shared with good friends. Sophie, Olivia, and Ed, please know that G and I treasure your friendship and generosity.

Ever since I've known my husband G, he has hated eating mushrooms. He would often grimace at the sight of them. Well, G ate all the dishes in this cookbook, including those with mushrooms, multiple times. I'm so grateful that he was open to learning to love fungi, willing to join me on my plant-based journey, and happy to have food on his plate, even if it was the fifth version of the same dish.

Finally, writing a cookbook can be incredibly tedious. I'm so blessed that PK and the little ones were always there to give me hugs and make me smile. They never let me down.

CONVERSION CHARTS

METRIC AND IMPERIAL CONVERSIONS
(These conversions are rounded for convenience)

Ingredient	Cups/Tablespoons/Teaspoons	Ounces	Grams/Milliliters
Cornstarch	1 tablespoon	0.3 ounce	8 grams
Flour, all-purpose	1 cup/1 tablespoon	4.5 ounces/0.3 ounce	125 grams/8 grams
Flour, whole wheat	1 cup	4 ounces	120 grams
Fruit, dried	1 cup	4 ounces	120 grams
Fruits or veggies, chopped	1 cup	5 to 7 ounces	145 to 200 grams
Fruits or veggies, pureed	1 cup	8.5 ounces	245 grams
Liquids: milk, water, or juice	1 cup	8 fluid ounces	240 milliliters
Maple syrup or corn syrup	1 tablespoon	0.75 ounce	20 grams
Oats	1 cup	5.5 ounces	150 grams
Salt	1 teaspoon	0.2 ounce	6 grams
Spices: cinnamon, cloves, ginger, or nutmeg (ground)	1 teaspoon	0.2 ounce	5 milliliters
Sugar, brown, firmly packed	1 cup	7 ounces	200 grams
Sugar, white	1 cup/1 tablespoon	7 ounces/0.5 ounce	200 grams/12.5 grams
Vanilla extract	1 teaspoon	0.2 ounce	4 grams

OVEN TEMPERATURES

Fahrenheit	Celsius	Gas Mark
225°	110°	¼
250°	120°	½
275°	140°	1
300°	150°	2
325°	160°	3
350°	180°	4
375°	190°	5
400°	200°	6
425°	220°	7
450°	230°	8

INDEX

ALSO AVAILABLE

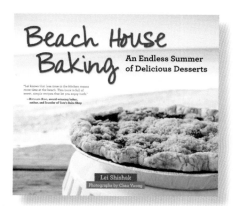